The School of Life:
Relationships

First published in 2016 by The School of Life
First published in the USA in 2018
This paperback edition published in 2022
930 High Road, London, N12 9RT

Cover design by Marcia Mihotich
Typeset by Kerrypress
Printed and bound in Canada

A proportion of this book has appeared online at www.theschooloflife.com/thebookoflife

Every effort has been made to contact the copyright holders of the material reproduced in this book. If any have been inadvertently overlooked, the publisher will be pleased to make restitution at the earliest opportunity.

The School of Life is a resource for helping us understand ourselves, for improving our relationships, our careers, and our social lives—as well as for helping us find calm and get more out of our leisure hours. We do this through creating films, workshops, books, apps, and gifts.

www.theschooloflife.com

ISBN 978-1-915087-13-3

10 9 8 7 6 5 4 3 2 1

The School of Life: Relationships

Learning to love

The School of Life

Contents

1   Post-Romanticism   7
2   Object Choice   15
3   Transference   23
4   The Problems of Closeness   31
5   The Weakness of Strength   39
6   Partner-As-Child   41
7   Loving and Being Loved   47
8   The Dignity of Ironing   51
9   Teaching and Learning   55
10 Pessimism   61
11 Blame and Love   69
12 Politeness and Secrets   75
13 Explaining Our Madness   79
14 Artificial Conversations   85
15 Crushes   91
16 Sexual Non-Liberation   99
17 The Loyalist and the Libertine   105
18 Celibacy and Endings   113
19 Classical vs Romantic   123
20 Better Love Stories   131

1
Post-Romanticism

To fall in love with someone feels like such a personal and spontaneous process, it can sound strange—and even rather insulting—to suggest that something else (we might call it society or culture) may be playing a covert, critical role in governing our relationships in their most intimate moments.

Yet the history of humanity shows us so many varied approaches to love, so many different assumptions about how couples are supposed to get together, and so many distinctive ways of interpreting feelings, we should perhaps accept with a degree of grace that the way we go about our relationships must in practice owe rather a lot to the prevailing environment beyond our bedrooms. Our loves unfold against a cultural backdrop that creates a powerful sense of what is "normal" in love; it subtly directs us as to where we should place our emotional emphases, it teaches us what to value, how to approach conflicts, what to get excited about, when to tolerate, and what we can be legitimately incensed by. Love has a history and we ride—sometimes rather helplessly—on its currents.

Since around 1750, we have been living in a highly distinctive era in the history of love that we can call Romanticism. Romanticism emerged as an ideology in Europe in the mid-18th century in the minds of poets, artists, and philosophers, and it has now conquered the world, powerfully (yet always quietly) determining how a shopkeeper's son in Yokohama will approach a first date, how a scriptwriter in Hollywood will shape the ending of a film, or when a middle-aged woman in Buenos Aires might decide to call it a day with her civil servant husband of twenty years.

No single relationship ever follows the Romantic template exactly, but its broad outlines are frequently present nevertheless—and might be summed up as follows:

– Romanticism is deeply hopeful about marriage. It tells us that a long-term marriage can have all the excitement of a love affair. The feelings of love that we are familiar with at the start of a relationship are expected to prevail over a lifetime. Romanticism took marriage (hitherto seen as a practical and emotionally temperate union) and fused it together with the passionate love story to create a unique proposition: the lifelong passionate love marriage.

– Along the way, Romanticism united love and sex. Previously, people had imagined that they could have sex with characters they didn't love, and that they could love someone without having extraordinary sex with them. Romanticism elevated sex to the supreme expression of love. Frequent, mutually satisfying sex became the bellwether of the health of any relationship. Without necessarily meaning to, Romanticism made infrequent sex and adultery into catastrophes.

–   Romanticism proposed that true love must mean an end to all loneliness. The right partner would, it promised, understand us entirely, possibly without needing to speak to us. They would intuit our souls. (Romantics put a special premium on the idea that our partner might understand us *without words* ...)

–   Romanticism believed that choosing a partner should be about letting oneself be guided by feelings, rather than practical considerations. For most of recorded history, people had fallen into relationships and married for logical pragmatic sorts of reasons: because her parcel of land adjoined yours, his family had a flourishing grain business, her father was the magistrate in town, there was a castle to keep up, or both sets of parents subscribed to the same interpretation of a holy text. And from such "reasonable" marriages, there flowed loneliness, infidelity, and hardness of heart. For Romanticism, the marriage of reason was not reasonable at all, which is why what it replaced it with—the marriage of feeling—has largely been spared the need to account for itself. What matters is that two people wish desperately that it happens, are drawn to one another by an overwhelming instinct, and know in their hearts that it is right. The modern age has had enough of "reasons," those catalysts of misery. The prestige of instinct is the legacy of a collective traumatized reaction against too many centuries of unreasonable "reason."

–   Romanticism has manifested a powerful disdain for practicalities and money. Nowadays, under the influence of Romanticism, we don't like such elements to be at the forefront of the mind around relationships, especially in the early days. It feels cold—un-Romantic—to say you know you're with the right person because you make an excellent financial fit or because you gel over things like bathroom etiquette and attitudes to punctuality. People, we feel, only turn to practical considerations when all else has failed ("I couldn't find love, I had to settle for convenience") or because they are sinister (the gold-digger, the social climber).

–   Romanticism believes that true love should involve delighting in a lover in their every aspect. True love is synonymous with accepting everything about someone. The idea that one's partner (or oneself) may need to change is taken to be a sign that the relationship is on the rocks; "you're going to have to change" is a last-ditch threat.

This template of love is a historical creation. It's a hugely beautiful and often enjoyable one. The Romantics were brilliantly perceptive about some facets of emotional life and were extremely talented about expressing their hopes and longings. Many of the feelings had existed before, but what the Romantics did was elevate them, turning them from passing fancies into serious concepts with the power to determine the course of relationships over a lifetime.

We can at this point state boldly: Romanticism has been a disaster for love. It is an intellectual and spiritual movement that has had a devastating impact on the ability of ordinary people to lead successful emotional lives. The salvation of love lies in overcoming a succession of errors within Romanticism. Our strongest cultural voices have—to our huge cost—set us up with the wrong expectations. They've highlighted emotions that don't tell us very much that is useful about how to make relationships work, while drawing attention away from others that offer more constructive guidance. We deserve sympathy. We're surrounded by a culture that offers a well-meaning but fatally skewed ideal of how relationships might function. We're trying to apply a very unhelpful script to a hugely tricky task.

This Romantic script is both normative and at points delusional. In order to be thought normal in the age of Romanticism, many of the following are meant to happen:

- We should meet a person of extraordinary inner and outer beauty and immediately feel a special attraction to them, and they to us.

- We should have highly satisfying sex, not only at the start, but forever.

- We should never be attracted to anyone else.

- We should understand one another intuitively.

- We don't need an education in love. We may need to train to become a pilot or brain surgeon, but not a lover. We will pick that up along the way, by following our feelings.

- We should have no secrets and spend constant time together (work shouldn't get in the way).

- We should raise a family without any loss of sexual or emotional intensity.

- Our lover must be our soulmate, best friend, co-parent, co-chauffeur, accountant, household manager, and spiritual guide.

Knowing the history of Romanticism should be consoling—because it suggests that quite a lot of the troubles we have with relationships don't stem (as we normally, guiltily end up thinking) from our ineptitude, our own inadequacy or our own regrettable choice of partners. Knowing the history invites another, more useful idea: We alone are not to blame; we were set an incredibly hard task by our culture, which then had the temerity to present it as easy.

It seems crucial to systematically question the assumptions of the Romantic view of love—not in order to destroy love, but to save it. We need to piece together a post-Romantic theory of couples, because in order to make a relationship last we almost have to be disloyal to many of the Romantic emotions that get us into it in the first place. The idea of being "post-Romantic" shouldn't imply cynicism, that one has abandoned the hope of relationships ever working out well. The post-Romantic attitude is just as ambitious about good relationships, but it has a very different sense of how to honor the hopes.

We need to replace the Romantic template with a psychologically mature vision of love we might call Classical, which encourages in us a range of unfamiliar but hopefully effective attitudes:

−   It is normal that love and sex may not always belong together.

−   Discussing money early on, upfront, in a serious way, is not a betrayal of love.

- Realising that we are rather flawed, and our partner is too, is of huge benefit to a couple in increasing the amount of tolerance and generosity in circulation.

- We will never find everything in another person, nor they in us, not because of some unique flaw, but because of the way human nature works.

- We need to make immense and often rather artificial-sounding efforts to understand one another; that intuition can't get us to where we need to go.

- Spending two hours discussing whether bathroom towels should be hung up or can be left on the floor is neither trivial nor unserious, and there is a special dignity around laundry and timekeeping.

Such attitudes, and many more, belong to a new, more hopeful future for love.

2
Object Choice

How do we choose the people we fall in love with? The Romantic answer is that our instincts naturally guide us to individuals who are kind and good for us. Love is a sort of ecstasy that descends when we feel ourselves in the presence of a benign and nourishing soul, who will answer our emotional needs, understand our sadness, and strengthen us for the hard tasks of our lives. In order to locate our lover, we must let our instincts carry us along, taking care never to impede them through pedantic psychological analysis and introspection or else considerations of status, wealth, or lineage. Our feelings will tell us clearly enough when we have reached our destiny. To ask someone with any degree of rigor why exactly they have chosen a particular partner is— in the Romantic worldview—simply an unnecessary and offensive misunderstanding of love: True love is an instinct that accurately settles on those with a capacity to make us content.

The Romantic attitude sounds warm and kind. Its originators certainly imagined that it would bring an end to the sort of unhappy relationships previously brokered by parents and society. The only difficulty is that our obedience to instinct has, very often, proved to be a disaster of its own. Respecting the special feelings we get around certain people in nightclubs and train stations, parties and websites appears not to have led us to be any happier in our unions than a medieval couple shackled into marriage by two royal courts keen to preserve the sovereignty of a slice of ancestral land. "Instinct" has been little better than "calculation" in underwriting the quality of our love stories.

Romanticism would not at this point, however, give up the argument quite so easily. It would simply ascribe the difficulties we often have in love to not having looked hard enough for that central fixture of Romantic reverie: the right person. This being is inevitably still out there (every soul must have its soulmate, Romanticism assures us), it is just that we haven't managed to track them down—yet. So we must continue the search, with all the technology and tenacity necessary, and maybe, once the divorce has come through and the house has been sold, we'll get it right.

But there's another school of thought, this one influenced by psychoanalysis, which challenges the notion that instinct invariably draws us to those who will make us happy. The theory insists that we don't fall in love first and foremost with those who care for us in ideal ways, we fall in love with those who care for us in familiar ways. Adult love emerges from a template of how we should be loved that was created in childhood and is likely to be entwined with a range of problematic compulsions that militate in key ways against our chances of growth.

We may believe we are seeking happiness in love, but what we are really after is familiarity. We are looking to recreate, within our adult relationships, the very feelings we knew so well in childhood—and which were rarely limited to just tenderness and care. The love most of us will have tasted early on was confused with other, more destructive dynamics: feelings of wanting to help an adult who was out of control, of being deprived of a parent's warmth or scared of his or her anger, or of not feeling secure enough to communicate our trickier wishes. How logical, then, that we should as adults find ourselves rejecting certain candidates not because they are wrong but because they are a little too right—in the sense of seeming somehow excessively balanced, mature, understanding, and reliable—given that, in our hearts, such rightness feels foreign and unearned. We chase after more exciting others, not in the belief that life with them will be more harmonious, but out of an unconscious sense that it will be reassuringly familiar in its patterns of frustration.

Psychoanalysis calls the process whereby we identify our partners "object choice"—and recommends that we try to understand the factors semiconsciously governing our attractions in order to interrupt the unhealthier patterns that might be at play. Our instincts—our strong under-currents of attraction and revulsion—stem from complicated experiences we had when we were far too young to understand them, and that linger in the antechambers of our minds.

Psychoanalysis doesn't wish to suggest that everything about our attractions will be deformed. We may have quite legitimate aspirations to positive qualities: intelligence, charm, generosity ... But we are also liable to be fatefully drawn towards trickier tendencies: someone who is often absent, or treats us with a little disdain, or needs to be surrounded all the time by friends, or cannot master their finances.

However paradoxical it can sound, without these tricky behaviors we may simply not be able to feel passionate or tender with someone. Alternatively, we may have been so traumatized by a parental figure that we cannot approach any partner who shares qualities with them of any kind, even ones disconnected from their negative sides. We might, in love, be rigidly intolerant of anyone who is intelligent, or punctual, or interested in science, simply because these were the traits of someone who caused us a great deal of difficulty early on.

To choose our partners wisely, we need to tease out how our compulsions to suffering or our rigid flights from trauma may be playing themselves out in our feelings of attraction. A useful starting place is to ask ourselves (perhaps in the company of a large sheet of paper, a pen, and a free afternoon) what sort of people really put us off. Revulsion and disgust are useful first guides because we are likely to recognize that some of the traits that make us shiver are not objectively negative and yet feel to us distinctly off-putting. We might, for example, sense that someone who asks us too much about ourselves, or is very tender or dependable, will seem eerie and boring. And we might equally well, along the way, recognize that a degree of cruelty or distance belong to an odd list of the things we appear genuinely to need in order to love.

It can be tricky to avoid self-censorship here, but the point isn't to represent ourselves as reassuring, predictable people, but to get to know the quirks of our own psyches. We'll tend to find that some ostensibly pretty nice things are getting caught in our love filters: People who are eloquent, clever, reliable, and sunny can set off loud alarms. We should pause and try to fathom where the aversions come from, what aspects of our past have made it so hard for us to accept certain sorts of emotional nourishment. Each time we recognize a negative, we're discovering a crucial association in our own minds: We're alighting on an impossibility of love based on associations from the past projected onto the present.

An additional way we can get at the associations that circulate powerfully in the less noticed corners of our brains is to finish stub sentences that invite us to respond to things that might charm or repel us about someone. We get to see our own reactions more clearly when we write things down without thinking too much about our answers, catching the mind's unconscious at work. For instance, we can deliberately note down the first things that come into our heads when we read the following:

If I tell a partner how much I need them, they will ...

When someone tells me they really need me, I ...

If someone can't cope, I ...

When someone tells me to get my act together, I ...

If I were to be frank about my anxieties ...

If my partner told me not to worry, I'd ...

When someone blames me unfairly, I ...

Our honestly described reactions are legacies. They are revealing underlying assumptions we have acquired about what love can look like. We may start to get a clearer picture that our vision of what we are looking for in another person might not be an especially good guide to our personal or mutual happiness.

Examining our emotional histories, we see that we can't be attracted to just anyone. Getting to know the past, we come to recognize our earlier associations for what they are: generalizations we formed—entirely understandably—on the basis of just one or two, hugely impressive, examples. We've unknowingly turned some local associations into strict rules for relationships.

Even if we can't radically shift the pattern, it's useful to know that we are carrying a ball and chain. It can make us more careful of ourselves when we feel overwhelmed by a certainty that we've met the one after a few minutes chatting at the bar. Ultimately, we stand to be liberated to love different people to our initial "types," because we find that the qualities we like, and the ones we very much fear, are found in different constellations from those we encountered in the people who first taught us about affection, long ago in a childhood we are starting at last to understand and free ourselves from.

3
Transference

Relationships are filled with curious moments where one or the other partner appears to "overreact" to a situation. These moments may quickly descend into bitter arguments, where the overreaction by one lover sets off a stern and heated response in the other. There may be very little search for understanding—and even less expenditure of generosity and sympathy. That's because we seldom recognize these overreactions for what they really are: garbled manifestations of a partner's tricky past that have not been fully understood or mutually discussed. It turns out that one of the keys to living successfully with another person can be to grasp just how much of a role the "transference" of past fears and anxieties plays in all of our behaviors.

Let's consider an example: You're flicking through a fashion magazine and playfully suggest that your partner might want to make a few experiments with their wardrobe. How about a different pair of jeans or a new T-shirt, a duffle coat, or platform heels? But at the mention of this possibility, your partner gets very agitated indeed: They scornfully declare that money is tight, they haven't got any time, they have too many clothes already and why are you deliberately annoying them by making vapid proposals like this? This response is very off-putting. You only made a perfectly reasonable suggestion and now they are declaring war. You didn't do anything. Their behavior seems utterly out of proportion with what triggered it. You may conclude, as you have done on other occasions, that in some areas the person you love really does seem "a bit mad." This conclusion, though perhaps depressing, also feels strangely satisfying. At least you know what is up.

But we are all a "bit mad" in ways that preclude such dismissive statements and demand closer and more generous examination. For all of us, there are situations and behaviors that can be counted upon to elicit swift and powerful responses that don't seem in any way in line with what is happening right now. Our behavior seems not to fit what is unfolding in front of us. For example, someone we love is going away for a month and tells us they will miss us very much indeed. They move to hug us. But far from feeling sad and tender, we just register numbness, pull away and can't say anything other than that the weather is unseasonably chilly today. Or we return home to find there is a bit of a mess in the kitchen, but rather than taking this in our stride, we start to shout at our partner that the house is chaos and life with them has become impossible. Or a friend is only ten minutes late for our birthday party, but we are compelled to send them a text calling them an asshole and asking them not even to bother coming.

These sorts of behaviors don't make any sense if we try to justify them simply according to the facts in the here and now (as we and their perpetrators are inclined to do). The clue to them lies in something known as transference—a psychological phenomenon whereby a situation in the present elicits from us a response—generally extreme, intense or rigid in nature—that we cobbled together in childhood to meet a threat that we were at that time too vulnerable, immature, and inexperienced to cope with properly. We are drawing upon an old defense mechanism to respond to what feels like a very familiar threat.

In most of our pasts, when our powers of comprehension and control were not yet properly developed, we faced difficulties so great that our capacities for poise, calm, and trust suffered grievous damage. In relation to certain issues, we were warped. We grew up preternaturally nervous, suspicious, hostile, sad, closed, furious, or touchy—and are at risk of becoming so once again whenever life puts us in a situation that is even distantly evocative of our earlier troubles. Perhaps a parent we loved left us for long periods to work abroad. They didn't mean to but the pain was so intense at that time that we reacted by shutting down our capacities for affection. Our way of coping was not to feel, to grow numb—a response that we keep producing even now, thirty years later, whenever someone we love has to go away for a time. Or perhaps we had chaotic, unreliable parents, whom we dealt with by rigidly organizing our room, arranging books by size, and reacting with alarm at the slightest bit of dust—and even now, outer disorder can usher in a panicky feeling within that everything is out of control once again. Or we had a sister who was always late to events that mattered to us, or a mother who was both humiliating and obsessed by fashion.

The unconscious mind is slow to realize that things have changed in the outer world but sadly quick to mistake one person for another, seeming to judge only by crude correspondences; "someone we love" or "a person coming to our party" appears to be enough to confuse us.

Because transference happens without us knowing it, we generally can't explain why we are behaving as we are. We carry years behind us that have no discernible shape, that we have forgotten about and that we aren't in a position to talk others through in a manner that would win us sympathy and understanding. We just come across as mean or mad. What we would ideally need is a guardian angel who can pause the present and carry our partners back to another time and place, to the moment when the neurotic defense that we are transferring originated. They'd be able to see the unreliable parents, the chaotic house, the loving but neglectful father, the fashion-obsessed mother, etc.—and might be appropriately moved by what we had to cope with before we knew how to.

The concept of transference provides a vantage point on some of the most frustrating behaviors that we ever have to meet with in relationships—and it allows us to feel sympathy and understanding where we might have only felt irritation. If we cannot always be entirely sane in our relationships, the kindest thing we can do for those who care about us is to hand over some maps that try to chart and guide others through the more disturbed regions of our internal world.

Key to building up such maps is working out where transference might be occurring. For this, we can rely on a range of "transference exercises." The most famous of these is the Rorschach test, devised in the 1920s by the psychologist Hermann Rorschach to help people to learn more about the contents of the hard-to-reach parts of their own minds. By being shown an ambiguous image and asked to say what it was, Rorschach believed that we would naturally reveal some of our latent guiding fears, hopes, prejudices, and assumptions.

The important point in any Rorschach test is that the image has no one true meaning. Different people merely see different things in it according to what their past predisposes them to imagine. To one individual with a rather kindly and forgiving conscience, the accompanying image (overleaf) could be seen as a mask, with eyes, floppy ears, a covering for the mouth, and wide flaps extending from the cheeks. Another, more traumatized by a domineering father, might see it as a powerful figure viewed from below, with splayed feet, thick legs, heavy shoulders, and the head bent forward as if poised for attack.

Building upon Rorschach's insights, the psychologists Henry Murray and Christiana Morgan created drawings involving people whose moods or actions were indeterminate. In one example, two women are positioned close to one another, their faces able to bear a host of interpretations. It's perhaps a mother and daughter, mourning together for a shared loss, one respondent might say, maybe they've heard that a friend of the family has died. Or another might assert: It's a housewife in the process of sacking (more in sorrow than in anger) a very unsatisfactory elderly cleaner. Or a third might venture: I feel something obscene is going on; it's in a bedroom, the older woman is looking at the younger woman's body and making her feel very strange but perhaps also somehow turned on. One thing we do really know is that the picture doesn't show any of these things. It simply contains two women, one slightly older, side by side. The elaboration is coming from the person who looks at it, and the way they

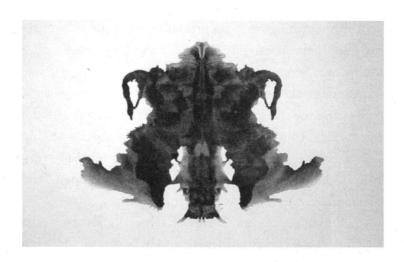

The Rorschach Test, created in the 1920s, uses abstract ink blots as a basis for psychological analysis.

elaborate; the kind of story they tell is by necessity saying more about them than it does about the image.

A third transference exercise asks us to say the first thing that comes to mind when we try to finish particular sentences. For example:

Image from the Thematic Apperception Test, devised by psychologists Henry Murray and Christiana Morgan in the 1930s.

Men in authority are generally ...

Young women are almost always ...

When I am promoted, what's bound to happen is ...

When someone is late, it must be because ...

When I hear someone described as "very intellectual," I imagine them being ...

Transference is not—as yet—an idea we normally employ as we try to make sense of some of the more difficult aspects of life around another person. That's because, unfortunately, transference doesn't announce itself to us as it should. The mind doesn't say to its owner that—at a given point—it is overreacting because it has met an old problem that used to be a source of much agitation. It can feel a little pathetic, or very vulnerable, to think that our current behavior is being driven by our 4- or 9-year-old self.

A sign of maturity is to accept with good grace that we might be involved in multiple transferences, and to commit oneself to rationally disentangling these, so that we will not need to keep making things tougher for everyone around us. The task of growing up is to realize with due humility the exaggerated dynamics we may be bringing to situations and to monitor ourselves more accurately and more critically so as to improve our capacity to judge and act on situations with greater fairness and neutrality.

4

The Problems of Closeness

In order to survive in the world, we have little option but to spend our lives being rather "defended," that is, at one remove from our more vulnerable sides, closed off from certain emotions, focused—in many cases—on not feeling.

And yet in relationships, quite the opposite is required. To be good at love means to have a capacity to reveal one's hurt, desire, and tenderness; to know how to be dependent and ready to surrender one's autonomy to another. It's quite a balancing act: great strength for most hours of the day, well-handled tenderness for the few that remain. It should be no wonder if the journey from independence to vulnerability can get rather fraught—and if the desire for closeness can be accompanied by terror and what looks like (but isn't really) nastiness.

Touchingly, when a relationship is beginning, we can find it daunting to reveal the depth of our affection to the other. We'd like to stroke their hair or whisper in their ear; we long to be important to them, but we hold back from a terrible fear: they might not feel the same way. Collectively, we have learned to be generous towards this fragile and very sweet state of mind. We tend to suppose that the fear of rejection belongs only to the opening moments of a relationship. Once we're properly together, surely, hesitancy and doubt will fall away. We've said we love one another, lived together, possibly for years, merged our finances and maybe raised a child. What doubt could there be?

Weirdly, though, the anxiety of being rejected never goes away. However reasonable we are on the outside, it still haunts us and brings multiple sorrows into our lives. It doesn't feel legitimate to still need encouragement and little signs of acceptance and enthusiasm, or indeed to have to give the same kind of encouragement to our partner. We brush it aside because there isn't a way to make it feel normal and natural to keep on requiring the same level of bolstering as we initially did.

However, deep within ourselves, we rarely feel sure that the other truly accepts us. There will constantly be new reasons to worry that they don't or won't. The signs that fire our doubts might look tiny. Maybe they didn't seem excited when we last had sex—which, in addition, wasn't very recently. Maybe we see them deeply engaged in conversation with a new friend; perhaps last night over dinner they didn't seem interested in the troubles of our workday; maybe they haven't said a word to us for the last twenty-two minutes. Despite the evidence of the years and a joint bank account, we are always on the cusp of thinking that this person doesn't love us.

However long we've been together, it can be awkward to request a clear indication that we are liked and desired. The sense that we're not supposed to need reassurance gets in the way of even admitting this to ourselves, let alone transmitting our request to the other in a frank but endearing way. Instead, our anxiety about being wanted might emerge in indirect and even disturbing ways. We hector and demand; we accuse and blame—tactics almost certain to push us further away from what we actually want: warm expressions of acceptance.

There are two classic ways in which our denied anxiety is translated into behavior. One is that we become what psychoanalysts call "avoidant." We go cold; we make it seem as if we don't care whether our partner cares about us. We make sure we have so much to do that we can't spend time with them—thus making it impossible for them to show, as we fear, that they aren't much interested in our company. At an extreme we might have an affair. This is an emphatic disguise and the strongest way we can send a garbled message: "here's how much I have to pretend I don't need your love, and a sign of how frightened I am of being rejected by you." An affair may in fact be a bizarre but genuine expression of love for one's partner.

The other danger is that we end up—as therapists put it—"anxious." Our fear of rejection leads us to be ever more demanding. We seek to control our partner, continually upbraiding them for minor failings. We're always checking on their performance of domestic duties, and we come down heavily on them if they don't stick to the letter of an agreement. We become their always-irked managers. We adopt these damaging, tyrannical attitudes rather than openly announce our underlying concern:

"I'm frightened that I'm not important to you and that you don't feel tender and warm towards me."

We should have sympathy for ourselves. Relationships require us to put ourselves in a very weak position vis-à-vis our partners, which can make us fumble for a show of strength and invulnerability. Our lovers access parts of us that normally stay hidden. Our love gives them so much power over us. If they ever want to use it—and sometimes they do—they know exactly where to put the boot in. It can be deeply frightening.

This aspect of relationships is even more difficult if our earlier experiences and childhoods have made closeness especially scary—if we've encountered people who have taken signs of vulnerability as targets. Our failures might—in the past—have been mocked, shy longings ridiculed, fears played upon. The prospect of having one's points of fragility exposed once again to another person can get linked to some very dark memories of humiliation.

We're not frightened of closeness because we're fools but because closeness involves genuine dangers. We're alive to how frightening love is at the start, and so we should admit that the danger is an ongoing issue. It is a challenge to be around another person who might easily hurt us—and to keep on in the relationship despite the fact they do sometimes use their knowledge to strike out at us. This danger isn't something that only a few unfortunate people are exposed to. It is a basic feature of every intimate relationship.

On the surface, both the anxious and avoidant patterns of behavior are horrible. In such states the person seems to be saying: "I don't care about you" or "I'm a controlling monster." But the controlling or distant person is trying, via their actions, to say something quite different. The deep message is: "I'm terrified you don't care about me"; "I'm worried you don't love me enough to go easy on my sore spots, so I'm putting on some armour or making a pre-emptive strike." What they say out loud sounds like a confident assertion of strength. More accurately understood, it is a deeply garbled, deeply misleading yet genuine plea for tenderness.

Tragically, our instinctive defensive moves are counterproductive. The person being cold or controlling so as to avoid humiliation ends up damaging the relationship they are actually—in a very strange way—trying to get to go well. They seek to avoid one problem—humiliation—and end up creating another one: a very confused, disgruntled, and annoyed partner.

There's a terrible poignancy about the way in which someone can be both nasty-seeming, utterly wounded, and yet very nice really. They sound like an angry lion but they are a scared child. It seems outrageous that these responses could spring from weakness. But they often do: It's a terror of being hurt that leads us to our worst outbursts.

If we're going to deal a bit better with the very common (and difficult) responses to intimacy, we have to start by looking with calm honesty at ourselves. A good question to ask is: What do we characteristically do when we need someone but aren't able to reach them? Do we withdraw, attack, or—this is so rare—explain our requirements in an un-frightened way?

The hopeful move is that we can learn to recognize our own and our partner's typical defensive maneuvers in our calmer moods. We can then see that when they retreat they're not really going cold on the relationship (though that's what it looks like on the surface). Or when they get controlling, it's not in fact that they are simply bossy; they are in a clumsy but maddeningly well-disguised way trying to secure our love and tame how dangerous it feels to need it. The move involves a shift in interpretation. We can replace a harsh view of what they are doing with a more charitable (and probably more correct) one. And if we have started from an understanding of our own tendencies in these directions, it's a little easier to grasp what might be going on behind the scenes with an infuriating partner.

In order to cope better with our challenges, we should embrace a different and more correct view of what our emotional lives are actually like. We should recognize how normal it is for a person who is reasonable and grown-up to also experience insecurity and to be in regular need of signs of acceptance, and acknowledge how timid we are about revealing this need.

Our trouble stems from a false but widespread idea of how robust and independent we're supposed to be. By this standard, it seems pathetic to worry that our partner might not love us because they don't like the way we cooked the chicken or because they just grunt when we ask how their day has been or don't feel like leaving a party when we're ready to go home.

Wanting little gestures of assurance isn't a mark of being infantile or an emotional wreck. It derives from something rather mature and admirable: We are aware that the other person's good will isn't guaranteed: they could indeed become disenchanted, and they don't have to be in a relationship with us. Anxiety is the price of the wise insight that their love for us is not an automatic given.

Ideally, it would feel normal to check up every day at least on one's partner's continuing good will without being seen as weak or "clingy." If we didn't feel ashamed to ask, we wouldn't have to resort to the strange underhand maneuvers of avoidance, hyper-criticism, and over-control. For these are, at root, strange strategies for trying to handle our uncertainty around our partner's love: an uncertainty that could be put to rest by a simple question, if only we felt allowed to ask it.

5

The Weakness of Strength

The faults and weaknesses of our partner can drive us almost to despair at times. It seems so unfair. We originally became attached to them because of their attractive positive qualities. But gradually the negative side of them seems to be most in evidence—at least to us.

Why can't they just be their nicer selves, we ask ourselves. Why are they so evasive around their plans; why do they show off at parties; why does the simplest administrative task defeat them? What makes it so irritating is that they could easily be different. They could drop their stupid behavior if only they bothered to try.

It is at this point of frustration that we can draw upon a very helpful idea: the Weakness of Strength. The essence of this idea is that a failing is frequently caused by an admirable quality. It is actually the nice things that we like about our partner that also—with painful reliability—produce the things we find most irksome about them. We become annoyed by defects that actually spring from virtues.

This vision of the fiendish connection between what is nice and what is annoying in a person was developed by the American writer Henry James. For a while during the 1870s he lived in Paris, where he got to know one of his literary heroes: Ivan Turgenev. James was deeply impressed by Turgenev's style of writing. It was full of hints and suggestions that were often left hanging in the reader's mind; there was never any sense of urgency, no desire to pin down once and for all exactly what might be going on. Henry James wanted to set up a lunch with Turgenev, but it proved to be almost comically impossible. The Russian agreed to come, then at the last moment sent word that he couldn't make it, but that he'd love to find another date. He was always enthusiastic to meet but dithered about settling a day, and changed his mind about which restaurant to go to. When they did eventually catch up, Turgenev arrived a couple of hours late. At first, James was hurt and bewildered—but then he realized he was encountering at a social level exactly what made Turgenev so entrancing as a novelist. The evasions around the lunch date had the same origin as his graciously open-ended and non-committal way of narrating a story. Being an impossible lunch companion was, James noted, a "weakness of strength."

This is a small anecdote with a large implication. There cannot be an ideal partner for us. Whatever we really like in someone will also make them a bit of a pain in other (but intimately related) ways. We could turn to a lovely new person, but their loveliness will unavoidably entail patches of awfulness. This is a strangely consoling proof that perfection is an illusion.

6
Partner-As-Child

If described plainly, little children's behavior looks outrageously mean. We kindly prepare their favorite lunch and they throw it on the floor in disgust. They kick our shins because we won't let them play with the kitchen blender. Interestingly, we almost never feel much bothered by this. We don't go around thinking they are vile and cruel, because we instinctively reach for the least alarming "translation" of their actions. They do not intend to insult or humiliate us. It's probably just that they haven't had their afternoon nap, or they are teething, or they are just back from kindergarten, which always leaves them a bit rattled. We have all these unalarming thoughts at the front of our minds, so we don't take their behavior personally. We don't feel got at or worried that we are raising a monster.

This is pretty much the opposite of how we deal with our partners. If they give us an underwhelming birthday present, neglect to put out the trash, or make a fuss about going to the theater with our parents, we assume that they are being intentionally horrible. They are doing these things to thwart us. We suspect they even take a grim satisfaction in upsetting us. And we in turn become enraged with them.

Ideally, we could reuse the moves we are rather expert at making around children. Perhaps our partner hardly slept last night. Perhaps something difficult is going on at work and they are embarrassed to tell us about it. Maybe they have a nagging pain in their left shoulder again. Such thoughts don't transform their annoying behavior into funny little incidents, but they do remove some of the personal sting. Our partner isn't actually being malicious. Our irritation remains at a manageable level. By drawing on our kindness to children we could learn to be more charitable to the childish aspects of a partner.

It sounds strange at first—and even condescending or despairing—to keep in mind that in crucial ways one's partner always remains a child. On the outside they're obviously a functioning adult. But the Partner-As-Child theory urges us to recognize that parts of the psyche always remain tethered to the way they were at the early stages of life. This way of seeing the person one is with may be a helpful strategy for managing times when they are very difficult to cope with: when there are outbursts of deeply unreasonable petulance, sulkiness, or flashes of aggression. When they fall far short of what we ideally expect from grown-up behavior and we dismissively label such attitudes as "childish," without quite realizing it, we are approaching a hugely constructive idea, but then (understandably though unfortunately) seeing it simply as an accusation—rather than what it truly is: a recognition of an ordinary feature of the human condition.

The therapeutic benefit is the observation that we are generally very good at loving children. Our ability to continue to be loving, and to keep calm, around children is founded on the fact that we take it for granted that they are not able to explain what is really bothering them. We deduce the real cause of their sorrow from amidst the external symptoms of rage—because we grasp that little children have very limited abilities to diagnose and communicate their own problems.

A central premise of the Partner-As-Child theory is that it is not an aberration or unique failing of one's partner that they retain a childish dimension. It's a normal, inevitable, feature of all adult existence. You are not desperately unlucky to have hitched yourself to someone who is still infantile in many ways. Adulthood simply isn't a complete state; what we call childhood lasts (in a submerged but significant way) all our lives. Therefore, some of the moves we execute with relative ease around children must forever continue to be relevant when we're dealing with another grown-up.

Being benevolent to one's partner's inner child doesn't mean infantilizing them. This is no call to draw up a chart detailing when they are allowed screen time or to award stars for getting dressed on their own. It means being charitable in translating things they say in terms of their deeper meaning: "you're a bastard" might actually be a way of trying to say "I feel under siege at work and I'm trying to tell myself I'm stronger and more independent than I really feel"; or "you just don't get it, do you" might mean "I'm terrified and frustrated and I don't really know why. Please be strong."

We'd ideally give more space for soothing rather than arguing; instead of taking our partner up for something annoying they've said, we'd see them like an agitated child who is lashing out at the person they most love because they can't think of what else to do. We'd seek to reassure and show them that they are still OK, rather than (as is so tempting) hit back with equal force.

Of course, it's much, much harder being grown-up around another adult whose inner child is on display than it is being with an actual child. That's because you can see how little and undeveloped a toddler or a 5-year-old is—so sympathy comes naturally. We know it would be a disaster to suddenly turn on the child and try to hold them fully responsible for every moment of their conduct. Psychology has been warning us for half a century or more that this isn't the right route.

However, we don't yet have this cultural backup fully in force to assist us in coping with a partner's childish sides. Naturally, the insight can't all be one way. A capacity for benevolence to the inner child of a partner has to be linked to a recognition that we will have a similar need to be viewed in this benevolent way at other points. We can take it in turns. We can summon up the energy to be charitable to the inner 3-year-old of the other—in part because we know that soon enough we are going to need them to do the same for us.

The way we imagine other people's minds constantly needs to be adjusted in a more compassionate and accurate direction. We have to keep reminding ourselves how frustrated, anxious, bemused, and self-critical someone who seems merely aggressive really is. Our lover may be six foot one and holding down adult employment, but their behavior may still sometimes be poignantly retrogressive. When they behave badly, what they don't, but should perhaps, say is: "Deep inside, I remain an infant, and right now I need you to be my parent. I need you correctly to guess what is truly ailing me, as people did when I was a baby, when my ideas of love were first formed."

We are so alive to the idea that it's patronizing to be thought of as younger than we are, we forget that it is also, at times, the greatest privilege for someone to look beyond our adult self in order to engage with—and forgive—the disappointed, furious, inarticulate, or wounded child within.

7
Loving and Being Loved

We speak of "love" as if it were a single, undifferentiated thing, but in truth it comprises two very different modes: *being loved* and *loving*. Part of getting better at relationships means growing a little readier to do the latter and a little more aware of our unnatural and dangerous fixation on the former.

We start out knowing only about "being loved." That's how it was when we were infants and others ministered to us. In our early years, we could do nothing but receive love; someone was on hand to comfort us, to play with us, to ask us how we were feeling, and to attempt as hard as they could to soothe our worries. For our part, we had to do very little in return. It wasn't our role to ask the parent how their day was or to suggest that, given how tired they were, they might like to go for a nap.

This style of relating to someone (with the other as our guide, helper, and servant) can (without anyone wishing anyone else ill) naturally come to seem the norm of what love should be. To the child, it just feels as if the parent were spontaneously on hand to comfort, guide, entertain, feed, and clear up, while remaining almost constantly warm and cheerful. And parents do their utmost to hide that there might be an alternative reality. They strive to suppress their moments of rage, despair, and indifference.

We take this lopsided view of love with us into adulthood. Our first (entirely unconscious) move—in our teenage years—is to hope for a recreation in adulthood of what it felt like to be ministered to and indulged as a child. In a secret corner of our mind, we picture a lover who will anticipate our needs, read our hearts, act selflessly, and make our world better and more complete. It sounds "Romantic," and yet it turns out to be a blueprint for trouble and disaster if we insist on it too fervently.

Perhaps you never had such a figure in your life, but let's imagine for a moment what a good mother might have been like: When you were a baby, she fed you in the night; you cried at 3 a.m. and she got up to comfort you until you eventually found your way back to sleep an hour later. When you were sick, she brought you egg and soldiers in bed. She was very interested in small things about you, like how you did in the school geography test or the graze you got on your knee in the running race. Nowadays, she wants you to be happy; professional success isn't the point. And when you mess up, your troubles are hers. She will put her own needs aside for you. She won't demand that you take her difficulties as seriously as she takes yours.

It's an extraordinary image of what love could be. And as adults, we can be forgiven for first demanding this sort of love from one another. However, we are likely to make a bitter discovery in the process: that we cannot now seem to locate an approximation of the love we knew as children.

We may rage against this and blame the other person for their inability to perfectly intuit our needs and love us enough, until the day we reach a true maturity, realizing that the only release from our longing for this sort of selfless one-directional love is to stop demanding it exclusively for ourselves and to learn—at times, when we have the energy and imagination—to give it to somebody else, to learn to make the same moves for our lover as an ideal parent once made for us. We won't manage it all the time, and nor should we be expected to. Adult love can only ever be a judicious blend of a request for, and an offer of, help. Yet it is not uncommon for a couple to seem like two small children who have been left alone in the nursery and are both wailing that they have been ignored, neither of them able to step into the adult role for long enough to build up the other—and then see their efforts returned. We should recognize how often relationships legitimately require us to put our own needs aside for a time in order to minister to another's suffering. That is when we will have finally learned the tricky task of knowing how to love, rather than simply to be loved.

8
The Dignity of Ironing

When intelligent and sensitive people—guided by Romanticism—come together in relationships, they tend to be agreed on an implicit hierarchy of what is and isn't important for the success and endurance of their love. They tend to be highly aware of the importance of spending time together (perhaps in museums or by the sea), of having fulfilling sex, of assembling a circle of interesting friends, and of reading stimulating books. They are unlikely to give much thought, however, to the question of who will do the ironing.

Part of the reason is that when Romantic writers explored the troubles of relationships in their works, they never talked about laundry. They tended to draw attention to an important, but notably limited, range of issues. The great Russian poet Alexander Pushkin depicted unrequited love in *Eugene Onegin*. Gustave Flaubert examined boredom and infidelity in *Madame Bovary*. Jane Austen was acutely attentive to how differences in social status could pose obstacles to a couple's chances of contentment. In Italy, the most widely read novel of the 19th century—*The Betrothed* by Alessandro Manzoni— discussed how political corruption and large historical events could overwhelm a relationship. All the great Romantic writers were—in their different ways—deeply interested in what might make it hard for a relationship to go well.

Unfortunately, there is a crucial omission in this catalogue. Little attention or enthusiasm has been directed at "domestic" things—a word that sums up the key, practical, recurrent questions of a shared life, ranging from responsibility for doing the shopping or cleaning the refrigerator to whether a cousin needs to be invited to dinner or whether to go on vacation to the same place we went last year.

According to Romanticism, these aren't significant issues. A relationship should be about elevated factors: intense passions, heroic loyalty, and integrity in the face of conventional prejudice. The daily tasks and squabbles of domestic existence feel, by contrast, unworthy of attention. Prompted by this background attitude, we don't weigh up domestic factors carefully when forming a relationship. We don't readily acknowledge that contrasting attitudes to such things as cleaning the bath or spontaneously inviting friends round for a drink will need to be handled with immense care and could otherwise wreck a joint life.

If a dispute feels high-status, we don't mind lavishing time and intelligence on it. We are more patient because we understand it's going to be difficult. (We don't throw our hands up in the air when we haven't found a new job or a better place to live after five minutes.) A Romantic attitude to love makes certain conflicts look minor—what level to set the thermostat to, or whether all the cutlery needs to match—so we flare up when they start to dominate our lives, as things like these inevitably will.

One strategy we might deploy to calm ourselves down is to tell ourselves that it's not worth getting worked up over a tiny detail. We should try to stop caring about whether "soon" means "in the next five minutes" or "in the next week" or whether it is disgusting (or lovely) to read the newspaper while using the bathroom. But this doesn't really work because—as we readily admit around the arts—details are crucial: they are the tiny points at which grand themes come into focus. We accept that a poet will agonize over the choice of a single word; equally, a whole attitude to life may seem to be summarized in the way a person squeezes a toothpaste tube or how loudly or quietly they close a door.

Characteristically, we don't "budget" adequately for such disputes. What is infuriating is not the difficulty in itself, but the difficulty being there when we don't think it should be. We haven't anticipated it, and haven't been educated to deal with it. Rather than ignoring contentious details, we should try to budget better for them.

The starting place is a frank avowal that living with another person is both tricky and important. Of course, there will be many small sticking points where the overarching nature of our two characters is inconsistent. But we would treat these almost as diplomatic incidents, requiring prolonged and painstaking negotiation. We would be willing to talk through with our partners the intricacies of how to share a comforter or organize a weekend with the same patient seriousness that diplomats devote to the sub-clauses of a bilateral trade agreement. For we would be sure, as they are, that a detail is rarely just a detail but is wholly worthy of extended discussion, eloquent exposition and much careful listening to the points of the other side. Unfortunately, our society has made this sound like the death of love rather than what it really is: a major help in making love work.

9
Teaching and Learning

There can be few less Romantic ideas than that you would like to educate your lover to be a better person. And yet, as we shall see, accepting a role for learning and teaching in love belongs to one of the fundamental principles of mature relationships.

There have perhaps always been—when you start adding incidents up—rather a lot of things about you that your partner seems keen to change. They notice how you put off ringing your mother. They want you to be more adventurous in how you dress. Three times recently they said they wanted you to get a grip on your finances. They've also hinted that they'd like you to take more of an interest in the children's homework and to help to host more dinner parties. It doesn't feel very pleasant. But, then again, they're not alone: If you are honest with yourself, there is plenty about them that you would—ideally—like to change as well ...

This all feels very wrong. The impulse to alter our lovers appears to run counter to the spirit of love. If we loved and were loved, surely there wouldn't be any talk of change? Isn't love about the acceptance of an entire being exactly as they happen to be?

The idea of wanting to change our partners sounds incongruous and disturbing because, collectively, we have been deeply influenced by a particular aspect of the Romantic conception of love. This states that the principal marker of love is the capacity to accept another person in their totality, in all their good and bad sides—and in a sense, particularly their bad sides. To love someone is, quite simply, according to Romantic philosophy, to love them as they are—without any wish to alter them. We must embrace the whole person to be worthy of the emotion we claim to feel.

At certain moments of love, it does feel particularly poignant and moving to be loved for things that others have condemned us for or not seen the point of. It can seem the ultimate proof of love that the trickier sides of us can arouse interest, charity, and even desire. Through life, we are always conscious that there are things about us that other people might not like very much—and we try to protect ourselves from scorn and criticism. What excitement then when our lovers seem to treat certain failings generously. When they find you shy at parties, they don't laugh—they are sweet and take your tongue-tied-ness as a sign of sincerity. They're not embarrassed by your slightly unfashionable clothes; for them, it's about honesty and the strength to ignore public opinion. When you have a hangover, they don't say it was your own fault for drinking too much; they rub your neck, bring you tea, and keep the drapes closed.

From these moments, an extremely unfortunate conviction develops around love: The idea that loving someone must always mean accepting them in every area—and that being loved must invariably mean being endorsed for everything one is and does. Any desire for change must, according to this ideology, arouse upset, annoyance, and deep resistance. It seems proof that there can't be love, that something has gone terribly wrong—that one should break up ...

But there is another more workable and mature philosophy of love available, this one traceable back to the ancient Greeks. This states that love is first and foremost an admiration for the good sides, the perfections, of another human being. Love is the excitement we feel when we come face to face with something that is strong, clever, kind, honest, witty, or magnanimous in another person. The Greeks took the view that love is not an obscure emotion. Loving someone is not an odd chemical phenomenon indescribable in words. It just means being awed by another person for all the things about them that truly are right and accomplished.

So, what do we do with weaknesses, the problems, the not-so-nice aspects? Romanticism tells us to embrace, even cherish them—all of them. We may do this with a certain number; a relationship wouldn't get off the ground if we couldn't. But at a certain point, we will reach our limit. Being told we simply have to love someone for all that they are, or else think of ourselves as bad people, is asking for the impossible. How could someone never want to change any part of us if they know us properly? Do we not ourselves aspire to change and improvement? Then why blame them for wanting from us what we at heart want from ourselves?

At this point, the Greek idea of love turns to a notion to which we desperately need to rehabilitate ourselves: education. For the Greeks, given that we are all very imperfect, part of what it means to deepen love is to want to teach—and to be taught. Two people should see a relationship as a constant opportunity to improve and be improved. When lovers teach each other uncomfortable truths, they are not giving up on love. They are trying to do something very true to love: which is to make their partners more loveable.

We should stop feeling guilty for simply wanting to change our partners, and we should never resent our partners for simply wanting to change us. Both these projects are, in theory, highly legitimate, even necessary. The desire to put one's lover right is, in fact, utterly loyal to the essential task of love—to help another person to become the best version of themselves.

Unfortunately, under the sway of Romantic ideology, most of us end up being terrible teachers and equally terrible students. That's because we don't accept that it's honest (let alone noble) to have things we might want to teach and areas where we might need to be taught. We rebel against the very structure of a lover's education that would enable criticism to be molded into sensible-sounding lessons and to be heard as caring attempts to rejig the more troublesome aspects of our personalities.

Instead, in the student role, at the first sign that the other is adopting a pedagogical tone (maybe pointing out something that we said rather too loudly at dinner, or mentioning a habit that is cropping up again at work), we tend to assume that we are being attacked and betrayed— and therefore close our ears to the instruction, reacting with sarcasm and aggression to the teacher.

Correspondingly, when there is something we would like to teach, so unsure are we that we're going to be heard (we develop experience of how these things usually go) or that we have the right to speak, our lessons tend to come out in a tone of hurried annoyance. We are frightened teachers, because we recognize that we have committed ourselves to pupils who don't even want to learn and in the process are ruining our lives as well as theirs (most pupils don't have as much power over their teachers' lives as they do in the Romantic scenario, which is why they are generally better). What might have been an opportunity for a thoughtful lesson will come out— under the panicky, scared "classroom" conditions of the average relationship—as a series of shouted, belittling insults met with by rebellion and fury by the student body. We don't use any of the techniques that we are careful to use when trying to teach a child or a colleague. Here we know to use extraordinary tact, to make ten compliments for every one negative remark, to leave ourselves plenty of time ... In love's classroom, we are the worst teachers we are ever likely to be.

Yet we should stop judging these faulty attempts at instruction so harshly. Rather than reading every lesson as an assault on our whole being, as a sign we are about to be abandoned or humiliated, we should take it for what it is: an indication, however flawed, that someone can be bothered—even if they aren't yet breaking the news perfectly (our friends are less critical not because they're nicer, but because they don't need to bother: They get to leave us behind after a few hours in a restaurant).

We should never feel ashamed of instructing or of needing instruction. The only fault is to reject the opportunity for education if it is offered—however clumsily. Love should be a nurturing attempt by two people to reach their full potential—never just a crucible in which to look for endorsement for all one's present failings.

10
Pessimism

Our lives are powerfully affected by a special quirk of the human mind to which we rarely pay much attention. We are creatures deeply marked by our expectations. We go around with mental pictures, lodged in our brains, of how things are supposed to go. We may hardly even notice we've got such phantasms. But expectations have an enormous impact on how we respond to what happens to us. They are always framing the way we interpret the events in our lives. It's according to the tenor of our expectations that we will deem moments in our lives to be either enchanting or (more likely) profoundly mediocre and unfair.

What drives us to fury are affronts to our expectations. There are plenty of things that don't turn out as we'd like but don't make us livid either. When a problem has been factored into our expectations, calm is never endangered. We may be sad, but we aren't screaming.

Unfortunately, our expectations are never higher, and therefore more troubling, than they are in love. There are reckless ideas circulating in our societies about what sharing a life with another person might be like. Of course, we see relationship difficulties around us all the time; there's a high frequency of splitting, separation, and divorce, and our own past experience is bound to be pretty mixed. But we have a remarkable capacity to discount this information. We retain highly ambitious ideas of what relationships are meant to be and what they will (eventually) be like for us—even if we have in fact never seen such relationships in action anywhere near us.

We'll be lucky; we can just feel it intuitively. Eventually, we'll find that creature we know exists: the "right person"; we'll understand each other very well, we'll like doing everything together, and we'll experience deep mutual devotion and loyalty. They will, at last, be on our side.

Our expectations might go like this: A decent partner should easily, intuitively, understand what I'm concerned about. I shouldn't have to explain things at length to them. If I've had a difficult day, I shouldn't have to say that I'm worn out and need a bit of space. They should be able to tell how I'm feeling. They shouldn't oppose me: If I point out that one of our acquaintances is a bit stuck up, they shouldn't start defending them. They're meant to be constantly supportive. When I feel bad about myself, they should shore me up and remind me of my strengths. A decent partner won't make too many demands. They won't be constantly requesting that I do things to help them out, or dragging me off to do something I don't like. We'll always like the same things. I tend to have pretty good taste in movies, food, and household routines: They'll understand and sympathize with them at once.

Strangely, even when we've had pretty disappointing experiences, we don't lose faith in our expectations. Hope reliably triumphs over experience. It's always very tempting to console ourselves with an apparently very reasonable thought: The reason it didn't work out this time was not that the expectations were too high, but that we directed them onto the wrong person. We weren't compatible enough. So rather than adjust our ideas of what relationships are meant to be like, we shift our hopes to a new target on whom we can direct our recklessly elevated hopes.

At times, in relationships, it can be almost impossible to believe that the problem lies with relationships in general, for the issues are so clearly focused in on the particular person we happen to be with—their tendency not to listen to us, to be too cold, to be cloyingly present ... But this isn't the problem of love, we believe. It wouldn't be like this with another person, the one we saw at the conference. They looked nice and we had a brief chat about the theme of the keynote speaker. Partly because of the slope of their neck and a lilt in their accent, we reached an overwhelming conclusion: With them it would be easier. There could be a better life waiting round the corner.

What we say to our partners is often quite grotesque. We turn to someone we've left everything to in our will and agreed to share our income with for the rest of our lives—and tell them the very worst things we can think of: things we'd never dream of saying to anyone else. To pretty much everyone else, we are reliably civil. We're always very nice to the people in the deli; we talk through problems reasonably with colleagues; we're pretty much always in a good mood around friends. But then again, without anything uncivil being meant by this, we have very few expectations in these areas.

No one can disappoint and upset us as much as the person we're in a relationship with—for of no one do we have higher hopes. It's because we are so dangerously optimistic that we call them a cunt, a shithead, or a weakling. The intensity of the disappointment and frustration is dependent on the prior massive investment of hope. It's one of the odder gifts of love.

So a solution to our distress and agitation lies in a curious area: with a philosophy of pessimism. It's an odd and unappealing thought. Pessimism sounds very unattractive. It's associated with failure; it's usually what gets in the way of better things. But when it comes to relationships, expectations are the enemies of love.

A more moderate, more reasonable, set of expectations around relationships would include the idea that it is normal and largely unavoidable that people do not understand one another very well in a couple. Each person's character and mind is hugely complex and convoluted. It's hard to grasp exactly why someone acts as they do. And, by extension, we'd be assuming from the start that no partner is going to have a complete, reliable, or particularly accurate understanding of us. There will be the occasional things they get absolutely right, a few areas where they really grasp what's going on in us; that's what makes the early days so charming. But these will be exceptions, rather than standard. As a relationship developed, we then wouldn't get hurt when our partner made some wildly inaccurate assumptions about our needs or preferences. We'd have been assuming that this would be coming along pretty soon—just as we don't take it remotely amiss if an acquaintance recommends a movie we detest: We know they couldn't know. It doesn't bother us at all. Our expectations are set at a reasonable level.

In a wiser world than our own, we would regularly remind ourselves of the various reasons why people simply cannot live up to the expectations that have come to be linked to romantic relationships:

One is dealing with another person

Much that will matter to us cannot possibly be in sync with another person. Why should another human being get tired at the same time as you, want to eat the same things, like the same songs, have the same aesthetic preferences, the same attitude to money, or the same idea about Christmas? For babies, there is a long and strange set of discoveries about the real separate existence of the mother. At first it seems to the child that the mother is perfectly aligned with it. But gradually there's a realization that the mother is someone else: that she might be sad when the child is feeling happy. Or tired when the child is ready to jump up and down on the bed for ten minutes.

We have similarly basic discoveries to make of our partners. They are not extensions of us.

The early stages of love give a misleading image of what a relationship can be like

The experience of adult love starts with the joyful discovery of some amazing congruencies. It's wonderful to discover someone who finds the same jokes hilarious, who feels the same way as you about cosy sweaters, or the music of Brazil, someone who is really able to see why you feel as you do about your father, or who deeply appreciates your confidence around form-filling, or your knowledge of wine. There's a seductive hope that the wonderful fit between the two of you is the first intimation of a general fusion of souls.

Love is the discovery of harmony in some very specific areas—but to continue with this expectation is to doom hope to a slow death. Every relationship will necessarily involve the discovery of a huge number of areas of divergence. It will feel as if you are growing apart and that the precious unity you knew during the weekend in Paris is being destroyed. But what is happening should really be seen under a much less alarming description: Disagreement is what happens when love succeeds and you get to know someone close up across the full range of their life.

Any upbringing will be imperfect in important ways. The atmosphere at home might have been too strict or too lax, too focused on money or not adequately on top of the finances. It might have been emotionally smothering or a bit distant and detached. Family life might have been relentlessly gregarious or limited by lack of confidence. Getting from being a baby to a reasonably functional adult is never a flawless process. We are all, in diverse ways, damaged and insane. The child might have learned to keep its true thoughts and feelings very much to itself and to tread very carefully around fragile parents; and in later life, this person may still be rather secretive and cagey in their own relationships. The characteristic was acquired to deal with a childhood situation, but such patterns get deeply embedded and keep on going. Our adaptations to the troubles of our past make us all maddening prospects in the present.

We keep supposing that our actual partner is unusually awful. We become preternaturally aware of their annoying qualities and we conclude that a terrible misfortune has befallen us. We thought we were getting together with someone wonderful, but they show themselves to be remarkably mean or difficult. We've been hugely unlucky. We have to escape this disaster. In our search for another life companion, we're deeply hopeful. This time, we will find the ideal person who will give us what we long for: love free of conflict and disappointment. Our Romantic longings don't give up: The problem was that person, not our expectations.

Yet being disappointing is not a specific failure of individuals: It is a universal phenomenon. A partner has their unique and specific problems, but anyone else will have their own different, equally maddening, repertoire of hangups, failings, and obsessions. What is genuinely special about our partners is that we have come to know their worst sides so well. The charm of a new person rests on the fact that we don't yet know them well enough to understand how they too could drive us mad.

11
Blame and Love

You and your partner are waiting, and waiting, at the airport carousel for your luggage. Other people are wheeling their bags away. Soon, you are the only ones left standing by the now empty conveyor belt. Gradually, a deeply unfortunate eventuality becomes clear: Your case has gone missing, along with all your clothes and some important documents too. Even if it does turn up eventually, it's going to mean lots of calls, explanations, forms, hanging around, and uncertainty. The already long day has taken an unexpected turn for the worse. At this point, your partner says something about how strange it is that baggage doesn't get lost more frequently, given the number of cases traveling around the world at any one time. The tone is observational and curious, the sort one might employ when trying out a hypothesis about the progress of the seasons. It is followed by a silence. And, suddenly, you realize deep in your heart that you are completely furious with them, furious that they could be so carefree and indifferent and ploddingly standing next to you in their casually fashionable jacket, so not-in-pain, when something like this has happened to you.

Moreover, an important piece of logic falls into place: Somehow, all this, the waiting around, the humiliation, the hassle, the hapless airline employees you're going to have to deal with, this is their fault. They are to blame for everything—even the headache that is right now clasping itself like a vise around your front lobes. You turn away from them and mutter, "I knew all along that I should never have gone along with your selfish suggestion of this expensive, boring trip"—which seems a sad, and rather unfair way, to precis an otherwise pleasant anniversary weekend in a foreign capital. Not everyone might quite see, or sympathize with, the connection just made. After all, your partner does not work for an airline, is not involved in baggage handling, and merely brought up the idea of a weekend away, to which you gave your mutual consent.

We are here circling one of the most superficially irrational, but most common and most important of all presumptions of love: that the person to whom one has pledged oneself is not just the center of one's emotional existence, they are also, as a result, in a very strange, objectively insane, and profoundly unjust sense, responsible for simply everything that happens to you, for good and ill. The world upsets, disappoints, frustrates, and hurts us in countless ways at every turn. It rejects our creative endeavors, it overlooks us in promotions, it rewards idiots, it neglects our talents, it delays our flights, loses our keys, and sends our luggage off to far-flung destinations. And, almost all of the time, we cannot complain. It's too difficult to tease out who is really to blame; or even if we know, we cannot say, for we would lose our job or be declared an upstart or impossibly thin-skinned.

The only person to whom we can expose the multiple grievances we accumulate is the person who is closest to us: the one we love. This blessed person becomes the recipient of all of our accumulated rage at the injustice and imperfections of our lives. It is of course the height of absurdity to blame them. But this is to misunderstand the rules under which love operates. We cannot and therefore don't usually get angry with the people who are really to blame for hurting us. Rather, we get angry with those whom we can be sure will tolerate us for blaming them. So we get angry with the very nicest, most sympathetic, most loyal people in our vicinity, the ones actually least likely to have harmed us, but most likely to stick around while we blame them for having done so. The words we mutter to our lovers undoubtedly sound mean. But let's at least remember that we would say them to no one else on earth. They are a curious proof of intimacy, a symptom of love itself—and, in their own way, oddly romantic (a detail indirectly acknowledged by their frequently sexual conclusions).

We can tell any stranger something reasonable and polite, but only in the presence of someone we really trust can we dare to be properly irrational and truly unkind. In part, we get furious with our partners because we assign them such a deep role in our lives. We have faith that a person who understands obscure parts of us, whose presence solves so many of our woes, couldn't realistically also be someone who would be unable to find a suitcase or in a wider sense fix our lives. Claims to this effect are confusedly interpreted as signs of a sadistic lack of affection and care—and have to be punished accordingly (we want to make them as unhappy as it seems they have made us). We exaggerate our partners' powers, an exaggeration that is an echo—heard in adult life down the decades—of a child's awe at their parents. When we blame our partners, we are remembering what it felt like when we loved a parent who could effortlessly swing us up to the ceiling, who knew everything, who could find Rabbit when it got lost, who always held the tickets and the passports, who ensured there was invariably food in the refrigerator, who controlled the world ... The partner, when loved, inherits a little of that beautiful, romantic, dangerous, unfair, trust we as children once had in our parents. At one level, the lover has learned how to reassure the anxious child in us—that's why we love them. But that source of strength also brings with it some very serious problems, for the primitive part of us insists on trusting them a little too much, believing that they actually control far more of existence than they possibly could.

On the other side of the fence, when faced with the outbursts of our lovers, we should strive (it is never easy) to remember that these attacks are deeply horrible symptoms of something really very nice: that we properly matter to another person, and that they have become deeply dependent upon us for their capacity to endure the humiliations the world daily accords them.

Irrational blame is at heart just a symptom of an intensity of investment in another person. We attack because we have richly entangled our deepest dreams and anxieties with our lover. It is because we are so very close to them that they draw us into very private zones of turbulence and distress—from which absolutely everyone else is excluded. That is one of the stranger, more unfortunate, and yet (from a very calm angle) almost flattering gifts of love.

12
Politeness and Secrets

For years, you felt burdened with thoughts, feelings, and opinions that didn't seem to make much sense to anyone else. You sometimes wondered if you were going mad. There were people you didn't like, but everyone else seemed to think they were great and so you held your tongue. You got anxious and uncomfortable on social occasions when everyone else seemed happy and relaxed. There were things you would have quite liked to try in bed, but they felt shameful and you would not have dared to mention them even to your best friend. You learned to keep secrets in order to be liked.

Then, finally, you met a very special person. What made them so special was that, at long last, you no longer had to dissemble around them. You could admit to important truths. You could confess, and be rewarded for sharing, your deepest self. It was a favorite game in those early months. You pushed yourself to go as far as you could go. The deeper the secret, the better. No area of the self seemed beyond investigation, no secret too shocking or explicit. You could explain that you found a mutual acquaintance arrogant, narcissistic, and mean. Or that you thought some supposed "masterpiece" of a book very boring. You could explain that you liked pulling hair during sex or had always been excited by ropes. Love seemed to be born out of this new possibility for honesty.

What had previously been taboo gave way to exhilarating intimacy.

The relief of honesty is at the heart of the feeling of being in love. A sense of mutual conspiracy underlies the touch of pity that every new couple feels for the rest of humanity. But this sharing of secrets sets up in our minds—and in our collective culture—a powerful and potentially problematic ideal: that if two people love one another, then they must always tell each other the truth about everything.

Then, inevitably, there came a moment of crisis. Perhaps you were in a restaurant, sitting with your lover, the special person who had joined you in your innermost convictions about everything. And now with characteristic confidence and trust—in the spirit of having no more secrets—you mentioned that you were a little turned on by the fascinating character reading a book in a corner table on their own. But, on this occasion, there was no conspiratorial smile and no shy but decisive agreement. There was no eager leaning forward, no whispered corroboration. Just a slightly pained, quizzical look from the partner, the trusted recipient of every secret to date.

We come up against a fundamental conflict within the modern understanding of love. Withholding a truth may feel like an attack on the integrity of the couple. Yet unfettered frankness, in time, strikes a fatal blow.

Total openness is a magnificent, and very touching, ideal for a shared existence; in the early stages of a relationship it is often a powerful source of delight and of deepening intimacy. But there is a problem: We keep wanting to make this same demand as the relationship goes on. And yet, in order to be kind, and in order to sustain the relationship, it ultimately becomes necessary to keep a great many thoughts out of sight.

Typically, we have an acute sense of all the dark and sly reasons why one person might want to keep something from their partner. We are much less conscious of how it might be a properly loving gesture to conceal certain things. Frankness appeals so much that we lose touch with the real merits of politeness. Authentic politeness isn't a cold mask: it arises from the desire to shield another person from certain genuine, but possibly nasty, elements of our own characters.

Certain facts about us—thoughts we've had, emotions we've felt, maybe some things we've done—would, if revealed, be profoundly disturbing to our partner. The hurt would be permanent and unfixable. Blurting them out in the name of "honesty" could actually damage love. (In the same way, parents must, out of love, carefully hide many of their own thoughts and experiences from their child.) The ability to edit and hold back is a central quality of the good lover, operating in careful balance with—at other points—their capacity for candor and revelation.

And if we suspect (and we should, rather regularly, if the relationship is a good one) that our partner might be lying too (about what they are thinking about, about how they judge our work, about where they were last night ...), it is perhaps best not to take up arms and lay into them like a sharp relentless inquisitor, however intensely we yearn to do just that. It may be kinder, wiser, and perhaps more in the true spirit of love, to pretend we simply didn't notice.

We should learn from the art of diplomacy, the discipline of not necessarily always spelling out what we think and not doing what we want, in the service of greater, more strategic ends. We should keep in mind the contradictory, sentimental, and hormonal forces that constantly pull us in a hundred crazed and inconclusive directions. To honor every one of these would be to annul any chance of leading a coherent life. We will never make progress with the larger projects if we can't stand to be, at least some of the time, inwardly dissatisfied and outwardly inauthentic—if only in relation to such passing sensations as the desire to give away our children or end our marriage, or have sex with a stranger. It is assigning too great a weight to all our feelings to let them always be the lodestars by which our lives must be guided. We are chaotic chemical propositions in dire need of basic principles to which we can adhere during our brief rational spells. We should feel grateful for the fact that our external circumstances are sometimes out of line with what we experience in our hearts. It is probably a sign that we are on the right track.

13
Explaining Our Madness

The Romantic vision of love posits the notion that people who are right for one another will have a deep, intuitive, and accurate understanding of one another. As a result, the Romantic attitude relegates explanations of why we act and feel and think as we do to the margins. Our partner is supposed to understand all the important things already.

But there is another, perhaps more helpful attitude to adopt. This posits that all of us are both deeply mysterious (to ourselves and to others) and also in many ways so eccentric and so intriguingly disturbed that it would be quite appropriate to use the word "mad" to sum up our nature. Furthermore, this theory argues that quite the kindest thing we can do for another person is to lay out with patience and imagination, ahead of any particular conflict or agitation, what our particular patterns of disturbance and difficulty might actually be. In a more enlightened society than ours, one of the first questions that partners would be expected to ask one another, and respond eloquently and undefensively to, on an early dinner date would simply be: "And how are you mad?"

A successful relationship always needs to be accompanied by a lot of explaining. This isn't because we are especially strange, but simply because everyone emerges as puzzling and warped at close quarters. We have tendencies, desires, inclinations, enthusiasms, habits of mind, and psychological zones that are very obscure. They stem from the strange interplay of the many factors that have shaped who we are: our unique intimate history of traumas, excitements, fears, influences, opportunities, misfortunes, talents, and weaknesses.

Properly seen, though, our madder parts are not actually bad or vile. They are just unusual and at odds with the normal picture of what an adult is meant to be like. But if seen generously, it's clear that they are not actually mean or cruel. The priority is therefore to try as best we can to help our partner make sense of us. Instead of hiding our peculiarities, we should (ideally quite early on, but it's important at any point) actively flag them up. We should admit that we're pretty odd in some ways and recognize that this can be alarming, until properly grasped. We should see explaining our stranger fears and desires in a way that's helpful to one's partner as a necessary, important, and genuinely loving part of being in any relationship. To be tolerable, we don't need to be entirely sane, we just need to hand out—in a good-natured and unhostile way—accurate maps of one's disturbances to one's partner.

A degree of self-deprecating humor is a central mechanism for the self-explanation of our troublesome sides—and is at the opposite end of the spectrum from the true enemy of love: self-righteousness. Humor rehearses a highly desirable and useful shift in attitude, for comedy is full of characters who could be seen as grim, frightening, or sinister but who we get to like because we are shown their foibles with a distinctive charm. Basil Fawlty would be a tricky husband to have in real life, but in a comedy by John Cleese he can appear as more than just an idiot; he can seem that much more tolerable being—a loveable fool. His vices are introduced to us alongside some deeply ingratiating qualities. The show teaches us to really like someone whom in real life we might have cursed; it is getting us to try out the unusual experience of simultaneously accepting that someone is crazy and still quite nice. We accept that Cleese's character is sly, selfish, mean, incredibly tactless, snobbish, and rude. And yet we like him. It's a remarkable achievement on the part of the comedy team—and is rehearsing a move we badly need to make with our partners; a relationship takes an immense step forward when the parties can move from viewing their lovers as irritating idiots to considering them as loveable fools.

In this sense, comedy is developing an idea initially sketched by Jesus Christ. Christianity introduced the notion that a person could be of low social status, of ignoble appearance, of poor education and yet be fully deserving of love and consideration. Jesus was setting an example of liking people who could be described as very unimpressive, because, viewed in a particular light, pretty much everyone can be made to look a fool. The question is whether we have to see foolishness as inviting derision and contempt, or might come to view it as fully compatible with tenderness and affection—in fact, with love.

To say that a work colleague is a bit of a Michael Scott isn't merely to point out that they are tactless and insecure. It's also to reframe those failings, because we come to feel tender towards Michael Scott too. We see his vulnerability—not just his idiocy; we become good at recognizing that it is his anxiety about not being liked or respected that leads him to do the deeply embarrassing things that make us laugh. For his part, Larry David is always getting angry and abusive. He is incredibly combative and rude to waiters; he gets into huge arguments with people at the dry cleaners; he tells his friends what he thinks of their partners; he speaks his mind, even when it is profoundly inappropriate. But at the same time, he's very charming. He's a successful man, he has a lovely smile, and he can be very sweet. So we're reframing the "grumpy old man" as "the charming, very engaging old man, who is frequently rude too." The comic move is to guide us to a benevolent conception of people—and hence to the parts of ourselves and those close to us that share the same potentially very annoying characteristics.

At the heart of much comedy is a brilliant act of explanation. The makers latch onto a character who normally would seem weird and off-putting, but they guide us to see that they don't need to be viewed that way. Instead of covering up or condemning the oddities, they explore the ongoing possibilities for love amidst the maddening flaws of human nature. For relationships to survive, it appears we too must take on—at key moments—some of the underlying perspectives of a great comedy writing team.

14
Artificial Conversations

Conversation is commonly held to lie at the heart of a thriving partnership. But our culture often has a skewed picture of what this might involve. We tend to adopt a Romantic attitude, which holds that partners ideally understand one another intuitively and see good conversation as free-flowing and spontaneous. It would feel cold and stilted to introduce rules, to resort to a manual or to take a class on "how to speak to your partner."

But the fact is, it is very normal to struggle in this area. We often end up sitting in glum silence, skirt round tricky things, or get into rows when difficult issues are at stake. A particularly poignant sign of the trouble we have with talking in relationships is the tendency to sulk. At heart, sulking combines intense anger with an intense desire not to communicate what one is angry about: one both desperately wants to be understood and yet is utterly committed to not explaining oneself plainly. It happens a lot, and it's telling us that, far from being easy and natural, good discussion in a relationship can be very hard to manage.

Good communication means the capacity to give another person an accurate picture of what is happening in our emotional and psychological lives—and in particular, the capacity to describe our very darkest, trickiest, and most awkward sides in such a way that others can understand and even sympathize with us. The good communicator has the skill to take their beloved, in a timely, reassuring, and gentle way, without melodrama or fury, into some of the trickiest areas of their personality and warn them of what is there (like a tour guide to a disaster zone), explaining what is problematic in such a way that the beloved will not be terrified, can come to understand, can be prepared, and may perhaps forgive and accept.

We're not naturally skilled at these kinds of conversations because there is so much inside of us that we can't face up to, feel ashamed of, or can't quite understand—and we are therefore in no position to present our depths sanely to an observer whose affections we want to maintain. Perhaps you have completely wasted the day on the internet. Or you are feeling sexually restless and drawn to someone else. Or you are in a vortex of envy for a colleague who seems to be getting everything right at work. Or you're feeling overwhelmed by regret and self-hatred for some silly decisions you took last year (because you crave applause). Or maybe it's a terror of the future that has rendered you mute: Everything is going to go wrong. It's over. You had one life—and you blew it. There are things inside of us that are simply so awful, and therefore so undigested, that we cannot—day to day—lay them out before our partners in a way that they can grasp them calmly and generously.

It is no insult to a relationship to realize that there's a shortfall of mutual eloquence and that this will probably require some level of artificiality. Our need for assistance is often especially acute around anger, desires that seem strange, and the need for reassurance (which tends to arise when one feels one doesn't especially deserve it). We should not feel that we are failures, dull-witted, unimaginative, or unsophisticated if we recognize a need to learn how to talk to our partners with premeditation and conscious purpose. We are simply emerging from a Romantic prejudice against doing so.

An artificial conversation can sound like quite a strange idea. But what it involves is deliberately setting an agenda and putting a few useful moves and rules into practice.

Over dinner with a partner, we might—for example—work our way gradually yet systematically through a list of difficult but important questions that we'd otherwise likely shelve or not find our way to:

– What would you most like to be complimented on in the relationship?

– Where do you think you're especially good as a person?

– Which of your flaws do you want to be treated more generously?

– What would you tell your younger self about love?

– What do you think I get wrong about you?

– What is one incident you'd like me to apologize for?

– Can I ask you to apologize for an incident too?

– How have I let you down?

– What would you want to change about me?

– If I was magically offered a chance to change something about you, what do you guess it would be?

– If you could write an instruction manual for yourself in bed, what would you put in it? (Both take a piece of paper and write down three new things you would like to try around sex. Then exchange drafts.)

Another thing we can do with a partner is to finish these sentence stems about our feelings towards one another— the idea is to finish them very fast without thinking too hard. What emerges isn't of course a final statement. But it helps to get awkward material into the light of day, so that it can be examined properly.

I resent ...

I am puzzled by ...

I am hurt by ...

I regret ...

I am afraid that ...

I am frustrated by ...

I am happier when ...

I want ...

I appreciate ...

I hope ...

I would so like you to understand ...

Part of the artifice here is to agree in advance not to be offended by what the other says, though some of what comes up is bound to be at the very least disconcerting. The idea is to set up an occasion on which for once it is possible to look carefully at genuinely awkward aspects of what's going on in the couple. The helpful background assumption is that we can't have a close relationship without there being a lot of sore spots on both sides. We're not (for a bit) going to be angry with one another. We're going to try to get to know what's happening.

We might also try out an exercise of fleshing out some sequences:

When I am anxious in our relationship, I tend to ... You tend to respond by ..., which makes me ...

When we argue, on the surface I show ..., but inside I feel ...

The more I ..., the more you ..., and then the more I ...

We're trying to identify repeated sequences of emotions, not to validate or condemn them but to understand. The premise of this artificial conversation is that (for the duration of the conversation) no one is held to blame. We're just learning to notice some problems with how we interact.

Relationships founder on our inability to make ourselves known, forgiven, and accepted for who we are. We shouldn't work with the assumption that if we have a row over these questions, the opportunity has been wasted. We need to be able to say certain painful things in order to recover an ability to be affectionate and trusting. That is all part of the particular wisdom and task of regularly having more artificial, structured, and uncensored conversations.

15
Crushes

You are introduced to someone at a conference. They look nice and you have a brief chat about the theme of the keynote speaker. But already, partly because of their beautiful suit and a lilt in their accent, you have reached an overwhelming conclusion. Or, you sit down in the subway carriage, and there, diagonally opposite you, is someone you cannot stop looking at for the rest of a journey. You know nothing concrete about them. You are going only by what their appearance suggests. You note that they have slipped a finger into a book, that their nails are bitten raw, that they have a thin leather strap around their left wrist, and that they are squinting a touch short-sightedly at the map above the door. And that is enough to convince you. Another day, coming out of the grocery store, amidst a throng of people, you catch sight of a face for no longer than eight seconds and yet, here too, you feel the same overwhelming certainty—and, subsequently, a bittersweet sadness at their disappearance in the anonymous crowd.

Crushes: they happen to some people often and to almost everyone sometimes. Airports, subways, streets, conferences—the dynamics of modern life are forever throwing us into fleeting contact with strangers, from among whom we pick out a few examples who seem to us not merely interesting, but, more powerfully, the solution to our lives. Oddly, the idea of a "crush" sits at the heart of our era's conception of love. Crushes can be funny or silly or barely last the weekend. They may seem trivial. But crushes deserve great attention because they reveal clearly and in miniature the three essential psychological elements from which our Romantic vision has been constructed. The central mechanism of love is the highly reactive union of restricted awareness of what the other person is really like, little opportunity to find out more, and immense optimism.

The crush reveals how willing we are to allow details to suggest a whole. We allow the arch of someone's eyebrow to suggest a personality. We take the way a person puts more weight on their right leg as they stand listening to a colleague as an indication of a witty independence of mind. Or their way of lowering their head seems proof of a complex shyness and sensitivity. From only a few cues, you anticipate years of happiness, buoyed by profound mutual sympathy. They will fully grasp that you love your mother even though you don't get on well with her; that you are hard-working, even though you appear to be distracted; that you are hurt rather than angry. The parts of your character that confuse and puzzle others will at last find a soothing, wise, complex soulmate.

When we invent an entire personality on the basis of a few small hints, we are doing something amazing, but not that rare. We are deploying around an actual person a natural inclination to fill in the gaps, as we instinctively do with sketches of the human face.

Henri Matisse, *La Pompadour*, 1951

This doesn't strike us as a grotesque portrayal of a person who actually has no nostrils, no contours to their face, and a nose joined to an eyebrow. We hardly notice, because we invent the missing parts ourselves. We instinctively build out from minimal cues. We ourselves are artists of expansion—although we don't give ourselves proper credit for our instinctive creativity.

The cynical voice wants to declare that these enthusiastic imaginings at the conference or on the subway, in the street or in the grocery store, are just delusional; that we simply project a false, completely imaginary idea of identity onto an innocent stranger. But this is too sweeping. We may be right. The wry posture may really belong to someone with a great line in skepticism; the head tilter may be unusually generous to the foibles of others. The error of the crush is subtler; it lies in how easily we move from spotting a range of genuinely fine traits of character to settling on a recklessly naive romantic conclusion: that the other across the subway train or sidewalk constitutes a complete answer to our inner emotional needs.

The primary error of the crush lies in overlooking a central fact about people in general, not merely this or that example, but the species as a whole: that everyone has something very substantially wrong with them once their characters are fully known, something so wrong as to make an eventual mockery of the unlimited rapture unleashed by the crush. We can't yet know what the problems will be, but we can and should be certain that they are there, lurking somewhere behind the facade, waiting for time to unfurl them.

How can one be so sure? Because the facts of life have deformed all of our natures. No one among us has come through unscathed. There is too much to fear: mortality, loss, dependency, abandonment, ruin, humiliation, subjection. We are, all of us, desperately fragile, ill-equipped to meet with the challenges to our mental integrity: We are short of the needed insight, composure, energy, and mental bravery. We haven't been presented with good role models; unavoidably, our parents were far from perfect. We are easily irked; we become angry instead of explaining our concern; we nag instead of teaching; we don't carefully examine our worries; we misunderstand ourselves and create flattering excuses for our failings. Under pressure, we become loudly assertive or unduly timid; needy or cold; controlling or evasive. These are the normal troubles of being human. We don't know in advance the exact details of another person's fragilities and inner disturbances, but we can be sure they will be there. In time, everyone will be seen to be radically unideal and will turn out to be very tricky to share a life with.

We don't have to know someone in any way before knowing this about them. Naturally, their particular way of being flawed (very annoying) will not be visually apparent and may be concealed for quite long periods. If we only encounter another person in a fairly limited range of situations (a subway journey, rather than when they are trying to get a toddler into a car seat; a conference, rather than 87 minutes into a shopping trip with their elderly father), we may, for a very long time indeed (especially if we are left alone to convert our enthusiasm into an obsession because they don't call us back or are playing it with distance), have the pleasure of believing we have landed upon an angel.

Maturity doesn't suggest we give up on crushes. Merely that we definitively give up on the founding Romantic idea upon which the Western understanding of relationships and marriage has been based for the past 250 years: that a perfect being exists who can solve all our needs and satisfy our yearnings. There is no one on earth who will not, on a soberingly regular basis, drive us to rage, desperation, hysteria, and, at points, a longing to run away or even die. And we will put them through comparable melodrama. It doesn't lie within our realm of possibility to be properly fulfilled or satisfyingly understood. We are not creatures designed for long-lasting cheer. Therefore, the choice of a partner is never one between contentment and grief; it is only ever a matter of choosing between pervasive misery and everyday unhappiness.

We should enjoy our crushes. A crush teaches us about qualities we admire and need to have more of in our lives. The person on the subway really does have an extremely beguiling air of self-deprecation in their eyes. The person glimpsed by the fresh fruit counter really does promise to be a gentle and excellent parent. But these characters will, just as importantly, also be sure to ruin our lives in key ways, as all those we love will.

A caustic view of crushes shouldn't depress us, merely relieve the excessive imaginative pressure that our Romantic culture places upon long-term relationships. The failure of one particular partner to be the ideal other is not—we should always understand—an argument against them; it is by no means a sign that the relationship deserves to fail or be upgraded. We all, necessarily, without being damned, end up with that figure of our nightmares: "the wrong person."

Romantic pessimism simply takes it for granted that one person should not be asked to be everything to another. With this truth accepted, we can look for ways to accommodate ourselves as gently and as kindly as we can to the awkward realities of life beside another fallen creature. A mature understanding of the madness of crushes turns out to be a wise backdrop to the tensions of long-term love.

16

Sexual Non-Liberation

We are repeatedly given messages that we live in sexually enlightened times, that we belong to a liberated age. And therefore, the implication is that we ought by now to be finding sex a straightforward and untroubling matter. We are not—after all—Victorians or prudes.

The standard narrative of our release from past inhibitions goes something like this: For thousands of years across the globe, due to a difficult combination of religious bigotry and pedantic social custom, people were afflicted by a gratuitous sense of confusion and guilt around sex. They thought their hands would fall off if they masturbated. They believed they might be burned in a vat of oil because they had ogled someone's ankle. They had no clue about erections or clitorises. They were ridiculous.

Then, sometime between the First World War and the launch of Sputnik 1, things changed for the better. Finally, people started wearing bikinis, admitted to masturbating, grew able to mention cunnilingus in social contexts, started to watch pornography and became deeply comfortable with a topic that had, almost unaccountably, been the source of needless neurotic frustration for most of human history. It seemed almost inconceivable how hung up our ancestors had been. Sex came to be perceived as a useful, refreshing, and physically reviving pastime, a little like tennis, and one that could sit perfectly well within the context of middle-class family life, once the kids were in bed.

This narrative of enlightenment and progress, however flattering it may be to the modern age, conveniently skirts an immovable fact: We remain hugely conflicted, embarrassed, ashamed, and odd about sex. Sex refuses to match up simply with love and remains as difficult a subject as ever, with one added complication: It's meant to be so simple.

In reality, none of us approaches sex as we are meant to, with the cheerful, sporting, non-obsessive, clean, loyal, well-adjusted outlook that we convince ourselves is the norm. We are universally odd around sex—but only in relation to some highly and cruelly distorted ideals of normality. Most of what we are sexually remains very frightening to communicate to anyone whom we would want to think well of us. People in love constantly, instinctively hold back from sharing more than a fraction of their desires and tastes out of a fear, not without foundation, of generating intolerable disgust in their partners. In the choice between being loved and being honest, most of us choose the former. But we are then burdened by a sexuality that refuses to stop haunting us. We suffer and yet may find it easier to die without having had certain conversations.

The priority seems evident: to find a way to talk to ourselves and our partners about who we are, and to tell one another (without setting off catastrophic panic, offense, or fear) what sex really makes us want.

At the heart of the dilemma is how simultaneously to appear normal—and yet achieve honesty about our sexual appetites. Our commitment to normality is important and touching. It means being (or at least trying very hard to be) patient, gentle, considerate, democratic, intelligent, and devoted to treating people with respect and loyalty.

And yet our sexual imaginations will always refuse to bow to normative parameters.

That we have to endure this searing division is the direct legacy of Romanticism, for Romanticism blithely insisted that sex could be a beautiful, clean, and natural force utterly in sympathy with love. It might be passionate at times, but it was at heart kindly, tender, sweet, and filled with affection for a single person. This sounds charming—and once in a while, for a bit, it is even true. But it woefully neglects some critical components of erotic excitement—and can't help but leave us deeply embarrassed about most of what we want. To start the list, here are just some of the unpalatable truths that stir in our minds:

- It's very rare to maintain sexual interest in only one person, however much one loves them, beyond a certain time.

- It's entirely possible to love one's partner and regularly want to have sex with strangers, and frequently types with nothing particularly to recommend them.

— One can be kind, respectable, and democratic and at the same time want to flog, hurt, and humiliate a sexual partner, or be on the receiving end of very rough treatment.

— It's highly normal to have fantasies—and to want to explore extreme taboos involving illegal, violent, hurtful, and unsanitary scenarios.

— It may be easier to be excited by someone one dislikes or thinks nothing of than by someone one loves.

These aren't just points of mild curiosity. They are fundamentals of the human sexual personality that stand in shocking contrast to everything that society suggests is true. The moment orgasm is over, many a nice person can be spooked by the need to effect a very drastic switch in their value system.

Despite our best efforts to clean it of its peculiarities, sex can't be nice in the ways we might like it to be. It is not fundamentally democratic or kind; it is bound up with cruelty, disloyalty, transgression, and the desire for subjugation and humiliation. It refuses to sit neatly on top of love, as we would so like it to. Tame it though we may try, our desires remain in absurd, and irreconcilable, conflict with many of our highest commitments and values.

We need to admit to ourselves that whatever the rhetoric and self-congratulation, sexual liberation has never in fact happened. Properly understood, it is about more than the ability to wear a bikini. We remain imprisoned, fearful, and ashamed—with few options but to deceive for the sake of love. True liberation is a challenge that remains before us, as we patiently build up the courage to admit to the nature of our desires and to learn to talk to our loved ones with pioneering honesty about the contents of our own minds—starting, perhaps (with the help of these words), tonight ...

17

The Loyalist and the Libertine

Long-term relationships almost inevitably confront us with one highly uncomfortable dilemma around sex. On the one hand, monogamy feels like a profoundly desirable and often default state, approved of by the community, religions, the media, one's children, and the ethos of Romanticism. It is a route to emotional closeness, a spur to coziness and a defense against jealousy and chaos. Yet at the same time, sexual exploration refuses not to seem in some way, on occasion, enormously compelling, obeying to certain deep-seated physical drives, and accompanied by the intense joys of breaking routines, kissing a stranger for the first time, and being for a while unencumbered by any practicalities or troubling emotional connections.

The dilemma has inspired an understandable search for what is discreetly termed an "answer," some way to reconcile two fundamentally opposed, yet highly necessary aspects of our personalities. For long stretches of history, the philosophy of monogamy had the prestige and appeared to have solved the matter. It was sanctioned by God and reinforced by society: Good people did not "stray." Then, more recently, accompanied by beguiling pop lyrics, festivals, nightclubs, and more revealing clothes, free love and polyamory entered the field and were presented as cost-free options that might allow us simultaneously to sample the pleasures of exploration and security.

We might in the abstract identify two clear-cut types of people—let's call them the Loyalist and Libertine—who represent extreme views on what monogamy or exploration might mean in a relationship. To the Loyalist, love is intimately tied to sex, so any adventures with another person (whether by them or their partner) must signal the death of love. It is simply impossible at once to declare love and a wish to have sex with a third party. To the Libertine, on the other hand, sex and love are radically distinct entities with an almost accidental, and partial, connection. A fling (or a series of them) can't say very much at all about whether one loves a partner—or, indeed, doesn't.

Both the Libertine and the Loyalist have taken hold of some important ideas. The Libertine understands that it is impossible to remain utterly faithful in a marriage and yet not miss out on some of life's greatest and most significant pleasures that lie outside the couple. The Libertine is deeply alive to the seductive powers of a sensory moment: another person's laugh or well-timed irony, a first kiss, a new nakedness—each of these high points, the Libertine recognizes as, in its own way, as worthy of reverence as more socially prestigious attractions, like the tiles of the Alhambra or Bach's Mass in B Minor.

The Libertine feels that it would be deeply unusual to expect people to grow up in our hedonistic liberated times, experience the sweat and excitement of nightclubs and summer parks, be bathed in images of desire and songs of longing and ecstasy, and then one day, at the command of a certificate, renounce all further sexual discoveries in the name of no particular god and no higher commandment, just an unexplored supposition that it must all be very wrong.

And the Libertine puts their finger on deep unreasonableness that seems to be built into our collective scheme of values. Typically, adultery is a lightning conductor of indignation—the one who strays is always to blame. But are there not—the Libertine asks—other, subtler ways of betraying a person than by sleeping with someone outside the couple? By omitting to listen, by forgetting to evolve and enchant, or more generally and blamelessly, just by being one's own limited self? Rather than forcing their Libertine "betrayers" to say they were so sorry, the "betrayed" might begin by being asked to apologize themselves, apologize for forcing their partners to lie by setting the bar of truthfulness so forbiddingly high—out of no higher creed than a jealous insecurity masquerading as a moral standard. The Libertine is rightly indignant that Romanticism has deluded us into thinking that it should ever have been possible for our needs for sex, love and family to be yoked together in a convenient (but impossible) contract.

For their part, the Loyalist gives proper weight to the fragility of the human psyche. They recognize that a relationship requires a huge quantity of collaboration and an accompanying feeling of safety—and that sexual adventure inevitably strikes a blow against these. It is very difficult to imagine one's partner entranced by another person's eyes, fascinated by the sensation of stroking their hair, and cuddling them in bed without feeling deeply rejected, bereft, and abandoned. Strictly rational arguments that compare sex to innocuous shared activities like playing tennis or hockey fail to understand the special place of sex in one's inner life—and ignore the fact that logical analogies with sport have little power in comparison to the oceanic currents of emotion unleashed by betrayal. Loyalists wisely know the corrosive effect of major concealments. They recognize, too, that for children the idea of their parents' togetherness can play a profoundly reassuring role, which can be tampered with only at great risk.

At the heart of both the Libertine and Loyalist positions lies a shared error. It is the belief that one or other of them is right and that if only the relationship could be built around their particular vision of life, mutual happiness would follow. The painful fact, however, is that both avenues are somewhat catastrophic. The demands of fidelity really do involve the loss of energizing, life-enhancing encounters with a range of sincerely thrilling people. Monogamy really is at times maddening and suffocating. Yet the option of infidelity, for all its charms, really does undermine trust and security, which are crucial to the functioning of a relationship and the mental health of the next generation.

The painful fact is there is no answer to the Libertine-Loyalist dilemma, if what one means by an "answer" is a cost-free settlement in which no party suffers a loss, and in which every positive element can coexist with every other, without either causing or sustaining grievous damage. There is wisdom on both sides; and therefore each side must involve loss.

There is, in a sense, only one answer of sorts, and it can be called the Melancholy Position, because it confronts the sad truth that in certain key areas of human existence, there simply are no good solutions. If we embraced the Melancholy Position from the start, we would need new, sadder wedding vows to exchange with our partners in order to stand a sincere chance of mutual fidelity over a lifetime. Certainly something far more cautionary and downbeat than the usual platitudes would be in order—for example: "I promise to be disappointed by you and you alone. I promise to make you the sole repository of my regrets, rather than to distribute them widely through multiple affairs and a life of sexual Don Juanism. I have surveyed the different options for unhappiness, and it is to you I have chosen to commit myself." These are the sorts of generously pessimistic and kindly unromantic promises that couples should make to each other at the altar.

We can remind ourselves that melancholy in relation to choice is not an aberration that visits us in this part of our lives alone: It is a fundamental requirement that keeps cropping up across the human condition. It was most clearly identified by the 19th-century Danish philosopher Søren Kierkegaard in a famously intemperate and darkly comedic outburst in his book *Either/Or*:

> *Marry, and you will regret it; don't marry, you will also regret it; marry or don't marry, you will regret it either way. Laugh at the world's foolishness, you will regret it; weep over it, you will regret that too ... Hang yourself, you will regret it; do not hang yourself, and you will regret that too; hang yourself or don't hang yourself, you'll regret it either way; whether you hang yourself or do not hang yourself, you will regret both. This, gentlemen, is the essence of all philosophy.*

The point being that around many of life's deepest themes, we just have no ideal option that represents a path to happiness. For this reason, when it exists, fidelity deserves to be celebrated as a high point of the ethical imagination—ideally with some medals and the sounding of a public gong—rather than discounted as an unremarkable default stance whose undermining by an affair should quickly provoke cataclysmic rage. The restrained Libertine deserves particular honor for their ability to both know the deep, genuine attraction of other people—and the immense excitement of adventure—and yet, with great inner sacrifice, hold back. Their full generosity may perhaps never be known by their partner, and yet it is an immense sacrifice for the shared good.

A loyal marriage ought at all times to retain within it an awareness of the immense forbearance and pessimistic, stoic generosity that the two parties are showing one another in managing not to sleep around (or, for that matter, in refraining from killing each other). That is something to feel properly optimistic about.

18
Celibacy and Endings

One of the more peculiar effects of Romanticism has been to discredit celibacy, defined as the act of consciously and willingly foregoing a long-term love relationship. Across much of history, it was taken for granted that married life would be an unhelpful burden for certain people: scholars, artists, and scientists could concentrate on their work; someone might simply have no interest in having a family or prefer to spend a lot of time on their own; one might prefer sexual adventure to a permanent relationship. The key point was recognition that marriage might stifle one's best self, and that wasn't something to feel ashamed or guilty about.

St Hilda of Whitby was one of the most powerful and accomplished women in the early history of England. She was a very senior administrator, running large agricultural enterprises; she was a management consultant to kings and princes. She was a leading educationalist. And she did all this while being noted for her good temper. She was also unmarried. It's not that because she was a nun she wasn't allowed to get married and so had to make the best of her work opportunities without a supportive home life. The line of thought ran the other way round. She was able to have a stellar career and achieve so much for the community because she was free of the demands of relationships and domestic life. Being a nun meant she lived in an efficient collective household—she would be supplied with meals, laundry, and heating without having to organize everything for herself.

It was an approach to certain kinds of work—intellectual, administrative, and cultural—that persisted for many centuries. In 1900, academia in the UK was still almost entirely a career for the unmarried, who lived in colleges, ate communal meals, had their laundry done for them by a university—and were betrothed to their work. If they wanted to wolf down their supper in eight minutes and then work through till one in the morning, no one would complain. The professors got a lot done.

The view was just that certain kinds of jobs require such effort and continuous devotion and loom so large in the imagination that we really shouldn't try to combine them with the duties of a relationship, a family, and the management of a home. To do them properly, we should live in very well-organized communes (like a monastery or a college), we should be single and we should socialize mainly with people who are involved in the same kind of work, because they will understand us and know how to offer us targeted help.

But Romanticism gradually made all these celibate choices seem strange. It pathologized the decision to remain single—and thereby ensured a lot of unhappy relationships that were now entered into by people who were not particularly suited to living in a couple but could not see viable alternatives outside of one. Romanticism made the idea of being close to one special other person in a long-term sexual union the very summit of life's meaning, and subtly discredited alternatives, like devotion to scholarship, science, art, politics, or religion— or a life simply spent having sex with a variety of people, with long-term affection being sought from friends instead.

Nowadays, anyone who lives alone and manifests no longing to be in a relationship is almost automatically (though more or less secretly) viewed as both pitiable and deeply troubled. It's simply not thought possible to be at once alone and normal.

This sets us up for collective catastrophe, for it means that a huge number of people who have no innate wish to live with anyone else, and are at heart deeply ill-suited to doing so, are every year press-ganged and shamed into conjugal life, with disastrous results for all involved.

So it is essential for the happiness of couples and the single that we regularly rehearse the very many good reasons why it must be OK to spend one's life without anyone. Only once singlehood has completely equal prestige with its alternative can we ensure that people will be free in their choices and hence join couples for the right reasons: because they love another person, rather than because they are terrified of remaining single.

Those among us who chose to stay single should not be thought un-Romantic. Indeed, we may be among the most Romantic of all, which is precisely why we find the idea of raising a family with someone we love especially unappetising, because we're aware of what domesticity can do to passion. It's in the end the fervent Romantics who should be especially careful of ending up in mediocre relationships: Relationships best suit the kind of people who don't expect too much from them.

Though it is a sign of some maturity to know how to love and live alongside someone, it may be a sign of even greater maturity to recognize that this is perhaps something one isn't, in the end, psychologically really capable of—as a good portion of us simply aren't. Retiring oneself voluntarily, in order to save others (and oneself) from the consequences of one's inner emotional turmoil, may be the true sign of a great and kindly soul.

The most logical response to really liking someone could fairly be to choose not to live with them—because it is almost impossible to cohabit and not eventually succumb to a degree of scratchy familiarity, contempt, and ingratitude. The properly respectful response to love may be to admire, praise, nurture—and then walk away.

All this isn't to say that being alone is without problems. There are of course drawbacks to both states, being single and being in a couple: loneliness in the one; suffocation, anger, and frustration in the other. We will probably be at times rather miserable whatever our relationship status—which is ultimately an argument for neither rushing too fast out of a couple, nor for feeling that one must at all costs try to belong to one.

There's an additional, related point concerning how long relationships should go on for. One of the big assumptions of our times is that if love is real, it must by definition prove to be eternal. We invariably and naturally equate *genuine* relationships with *lifelong* relationships.

And therefore it seems almost impossible for us to interpret the ending of a union after only a limited period—a few weeks, or five or ten years, or anything short of our or the partner's death-date—as something other than a problem, a failure, and an emotional catastrophe that is someone's fault, probably our own. There are people desperate that they have failed because their relationships have lasted only thirty-two years. We appear fundamentally unable to trust that a relationship could be at once sincere, meaningful, and important— and yet at the same time fairly and guiltlessly limited in its duration.

There are, of course, a few very good reasons for our collective valorization of the lifelong love story. A great many of the pleasures and virtues of relationships do only reveal themselves over time, once trust has been established and loyalty fully demonstrated. When two people know it is forever, they will work harder than at anything else in their lives; there is no option to avoid some necessary but unpleasant issues; they will do their utmost to understand the mysteries of the other's psyche; they will show reserves of tenderness and vulnerability they wouldn't ever otherwise have accessed. They will learn to apologize and reach a modesty about their own shortcomings. They will grow up. And in the meantime, day to day, they will sample the modest but genuine pleasures of cozy Sunday evenings together and shared walks in parks. Not least, children always benefit. But it's because the charms of the long-term are so clear in our collective imaginations that we should acknowledge the danger of cruelly and normatively suppressing all the legitimate claims of short-term love, an arrangement that deserves to be interpreted not merely as a pathologically stunted or interrupted version of a long-term union, but as a state with distinctive virtues of its own, one that we might rationally choose from the outset, knowing from the start that it would be better for both parties if there was a termination point more or less in view.

So much can go right with short-term love:

—   When two people know they don't own one another, they are extremely careful to earn each other's respect on a daily basis. Knowing someone could leave us at any time isn't only grounds for insecurity, it's a constant catalyst for tender appreciation.

—   When it isn't forever, we can let differences lie. If the journey is to be long, absolute alignment can feel key. But when the time is short, we are readier to surrender our entrenched positions, to be unthreatened by novelties and dissonances. The distinctive things they have in their refrigerator and the peculiar things they like to watch and listen to aren't affronts to our values, they are unthreatening invitations to expand our personalities.

—   Very few of us come out well from being closely observed, twenty-four hours a day, in a limited space. These may simply not be the preconditions for getting the best out of some of us. Our interesting and generous sides may need, in order to emerge, our own bedroom and bathroom, quite a few hours to ourselves, some space to read and think and a series of mealtimes alone staring rather blankly out of the window without having to explain how we feel. It's not a sign of evil, just what we require to be the best version of ourselves.

—   What makes people difficult and dooms relationships is almost never the people involved. It's what we are trying to do with them. Inviting someone to marry you is really not a very kind thing to do to someone you love, because it's going to drag the beloved into a range of rather unpleasant and challenging things: doing the accounts with you, meeting your family regularly, seeing you exhausted and bleary-eyed after work, keeping the living room tidy, bringing up a child. To really love someone—that is, to wish the best for someone—might more fairly mean foregrounding your best qualities for a few ecstatic months, then mutually and tenderly parting at checkin.

— Long-term relationships reward some qualities—especially the administrative ones—but obscure others, for example, those related to skills at having interesting speculative conversations about ethics or psychology late into the night. It should be no insult to determine that some people simply won't be able to shine in the conditions of long-term love, and that it is very kindly playing up to their strengths to leave them long before we ever need to try to arrange a cutlery drawer with them.

— We should beware of succumbing to the debilitating feeling that because it didn't last forever, it can have been nothing at all. In other areas of life, we know that "going on for ever" isn't the ideal (even when something is very good). We don't necessarily think we have to stay in the same house all our lives, though we might really like the one we are in; we're not betraying it or destroying it when we recognize that for a range of reasons it would be wisest to go elsewhere.

— We need to have an account of love that allows that a relationship can end without anyone having viciously or pathologically killed it prematurely, for only against such a backdrop can we reduce the debilitating quantity of bitterness, guilt, and blame otherwise in circulation. How we see the endings of love depends to a critical extent on what our societies tell us is "normal." If it was meant to last forever, every ending would by necessity have to be described as a horrifying failure. But if we allow imaginative space for short-term love, then an ending may signal a deeper loyalty, not to the setting up of a home and domestic routines, but to transitory pleasures; we'll walk away with a fair and generous sense of all that has been preserved and enhanced by the relationship not being forced to last forever.

19

Classical vs Romantic

We may not be used to conceiving of ourselves in these terms, but the labels Romantic and Classical usefully bring into focus some of the central themes of how we think about love. Though they coexist to some extent in each of us, we all tend to be more one than the other. What follows are a few of the central contrasting characteristics of Romantic and Classical attitudes to love and relationships.

1. Intuition vs Analysis

Romantics relish the ways love can seem slightly to defy rational explanation. They are enthusiastic about feelings and wary of the intellect as a guide to life. They like the notion that you just know by instinct that someone is right for you, or that your feelings simply tell you that a relationship is over. In their eyes, it is cold and even a bit cruel to probe a decision or a mood too hard. In particular, they think one shouldn't strive to take apart emotions. They have a deep respect for high-flown vague language and obscure modes of expression, which seem to them to hint at valuable yet ineffable aspects of love and closeness. They don't think it's a particularly good idea to draw up lists of pros or cons or try to spell out exactly what may be going well or badly in a relationship.

Classicists, on the other hand, are wary of intuition. They tend to have learned, often through bitter experience, how misguided and deluded their own feelings may be and hence look rather skeptically and caustically upon them. They see no conflict between loving someone and asking probing questions about why they do. They favor clear modes of expression (even about rare and evanescent emotions, like looking into their partner's eyes) and like language that an intelligent 12-year-old could understand.

2. Spontaneity vs Education

Romantics have often been wary of teaching and instruction. They think that the best things in a relationship happen spontaneously; you don't need to learn how to relate; you should follow your impulses. The idea that people might want to think rationally and exhaustively about who to be with or how to deal with the laundry or whether to have children strikes the Romantic as a misguided intrusion of education into things that should be natural (they like the notion of "love at first sight").

Those of a Classical temperament don't necessarily respect the current education system as we know it, but the abstract idea of education seems to them very important. They believe that training is vital if we are to avoid making too many mistakes in our emotional lives. The Classically minded person sees education as perfectly placed to make good the shortfalls of our wayward natures. We might need to learn how to understand our own needs, how to compromise and how to talk to, or have good-enough sex with, our partners.

3. Honesty vs Politeness

The Romantic person is devoted to saying what they think or feel. They are allergic to the idea of being fake or of having secrets. Authenticity is vital. They imagine politeness as a very dull lid that suppresses what really matters—and hence as being at odds with their idea of what a relationship should be like.

The Classical person reveres politeness as a very important lid that suppresses what might destroy us. They believe deeply in getting on around other people. It is not that they are afraid of ruffling their partner's feathers per se—but they just doubt whether it is usually a very constructive move and they are not interested in merely symbolic victories. They would prefer to have civil relations with the person they live with rather than always tell them emphatically what is on their mind. They accept an important role for secrets and white lies in love.

4. Idealism vs Realism

The Romantic is excited by how things might ideally be, and judges the current state of a relationship by the standard of a better imagined alternative. Most of the time, the current state of things arouses them to intense disappointment and anger as they consider the compromises, the imperfect degree of closeness, and times of frustration or distance. They can get furious with their partners for letting them down and surprised and outraged by evidence of petty selfishness, less than total frankness, or any hint of sexual interests not wholly focused on them.

For their part, the Classical person doesn't feel that ideal scenarios are worth much attention. They are very concerned to mitigate the downside. They are aware that most things could be a lot worse. Before condemning a relationship, they consider the ways relationships normally play out and may regard their union as bearable, under the circumstances. Their view of themselves and their partner is fundamentally rather dark. They believe that everyone is probably slightly more mixed up and selfish than they seem. They assume that both they and their partner (and anyone else they might conceivably have a relationship with in the future) will have some dangerous impulses, strange quirks of lust and coldness, and hard-to-control drives. When bad behavior manifests itself, they simply feel this is what humans are prone to. High ideals strike them as unhelpful.

5. Earnestness vs Irony

The Romantic's attention is fixed on their search for the ideal relationship; they like to think that anything that bothers them about their partner can be changed. They therefore resist the deflationary call of ironic humor (which says in many different guises—"of course we're both pretty messed up really") because it seems defeatist.

The Classical conviction is not that their relationship (or their partner or indeed their own personality) is already wonderful; far from it. But rather what they sense is that a cheerful mood is a good starting point for coping in a radically imperfect relationship, which they accept as pretty much the only kind of relationship there really ever is. The priority is not to get everything perfect, and not to give up, despair or run away. Ironic humor is a standard recourse for the Classically minded lover because it emerges from the constant collision between how one would like things to be—and how it seems they in fact are. These types appreciate quite a bit of gallows humor around their relationships.

6. The Rare vs The Everyday

Romantics rebel against the ordinary. They are keen on the exotic and the rare. They like the thought that their relationship is special. They set particular store on doing unusual things. They don't think much of routine in domestic life. They want heroism, excitement, and an end to boredom. They don't like the idea of money being an important factor in whether a relationship goes well or not.

The Classical personality welcomes routine as a defense against chaos. They are familiar enough with extremes as to welcome things that are a little boring. They can see the charm of doing the laundry. They embrace the thought that being in a relationship has a fair few things in common with running a small business.

7. Purity vs Ambivalence

The Romantic is drawn to either wholehearted endorsement or total rejection. Ideally, partners should love everything about each other—or break up. The Romantic is dismayed by compromise. In a domestic argument it is very important for the Romantic to feel they are right; actually resolving an issue in collaboration with their partner doesn't excite them to the same degree.

The Classical person takes the view that very few things, and no people (especially themselves or their partner), are either wholly good or entirely bad. They assume that there is likely to be some worth in opposing ideas and something to be learned from both sides. It is Classical to think that your partner, though overall very nice, might in certain areas hold views you find deeply unpalatable and a little absurd.

Both Romantic and Classical orientations have important truths to impart. Neither is wholly right or wrong. They need to be balanced. And none of us are in any case ever simply one or the other. But because a good relationship requires a judicious balance of both, at this point in history, it might be the Classical attitude whose distinctive claims and wisdom we need to listen to most intently. It is a mode of approaching life that is ripe for rediscovery.

20
Better Love Stories

We don't particularly notice it day to day, but the stories our culture presents us with concerning love and relationships—via movies, songs, novels, and adverts—have a major subterranean influence on how we think and feel. They shape our sense of what is normal and hence of what is troublingly abnormal; they seed certain hopes and expectations and foster particular opportunities for disappointment, indignation, or alarm.

It's pretty much a given that any society will tell itself stories about love. The question at any point is how helpful the predominant ones might be, whether they might be geared to assisting people to make a better go of love, or—inadvertently—may be making it harder to cope well with the realities of coupledom.

There are seemingly far too many bad love stories out there—by which one means stories that do not give us a correct map of love, that leave us unprepared to deal adequately with the tensions of relationships. In moments of acute distress, our grief is too often complicated by a sense that things have become, for us alone, unusually and perversely difficult. Not only are we suffering, but it seems that our suffering has no equivalent in the lives of other more or less sane people.

As we have seen, our attitudes to our own love lives are in large part formed by the tradition of the Romantic love story (which nowadays is advanced not only in books but also in video, music, and advertising). The narrative arts of the Romantic love story have unwittingly constructed a difficult template of expectations of what relationships are supposed to be like—in the light of which our own love lives often look grievously and deeply unsatisfying. We break up or feel ourselves cursed in significant part because we are exposed to the wrong stories.

If this "wrong" kind is to be termed Romantic, then the right kind—of which there are so few—might, as we've seen, be deemed Classical. Here would be some of the differences:

The Plot

In the archetypal Romantic story, the drama hinges entirely on how a couple get together: the "love story" is no such thing, it is merely the account of how love begins. All sorts of obstacles are placed in the way of love's birth, and the interest lies in watching their steady overcoming: There might be misunderstandings, bad luck, prejudice, war, a rival, a fear of intimacy, or—most poignantly— shyness ... But in the end, after tribulations, the right people will eventually get into couples. Love begins—and the story must end.

But in the Classical story, that wiser, less imme-diately seductive genre, the real problem isn't finding a partner, it is tolerating them, and being tolerated, over time. It knows that the start of relationships is not the high point that Romantic culture assumes; it is merely the first step of a far longer, more ambivalent, and yet quietly far more heroic journey—on which it directs its intelligence and scrutiny.

Work

In the Romantic story, the characters may have jobs, but on the whole they have little impact on their psyches. Work goes on somewhere else. What one does for a living is not thought relevant to an understanding of love.

But in the Classical story, we see that work is in fact a huge part of life, with an overwhelming role in shaping our relationships. Whatever our emotional dispositions, it is the stress of work that ends up generating a sizeable share of the trouble lovers will have with each other.

Children

In the Romantic story, children are incidental, sweet symbols of mutual love, or naughty in an endearing way. They rarely cry, take up little time, and are generally wise, exhibiting a native, unschooled intelligence.

In the Classical story, we see that relationships are fundamentally oriented towards the having and raising of children—and at the same time, that children place the couple under unbearable strains. They can kill the passion that made them possible. Life moves from the sublime to the quotidian. There are toys in the living room, pieces of chicken under the table, and no time to talk. Everyone is always tired. This too is love.

Practicalities

In the Romantic story, we have only a hazy idea of who does the housework. It is not seen as relevant to a relationship. Domesticity is a corrupting force and people who care a lot about it are likely to be unhappy in their relationships. We are unlikely to learn a great deal concerning a couple's thinking on homework or television for the under-4s.

In the Classical story, relationships are understood to be institutions, not just emotions. Part of their rationale is to enable two people to function as a joint economic unit for the education of the next generation. This is in no way banal. There are opportunities for genuine heroism. Especially around laundry.

Sex

In the Romantic story, sex and love are shown to belong together. The high point of love is intercourse. Adultery, in the Romantic view, is therefore fatal: if you were with the right person, you could never be unfaithful.

The Classical story knows that long-term love may not set up the best preconditions for sex. The Classical attitude sees love and sex as distinct and at times divergent themes in life. And therefore sexual problems do not in themselves indicate that a relationship is, overall, a disaster ...

Compatibility

The Romantic story cares about the harmony (or lack of it) between the souls of the protagonists. It believes that the fundamental challenge of Romantic life is to find someone who completely understands us and with whom there need never be any more secrets. It believes that love is finding your other half, your spiritual twin. Love is not about training or education; it is an instinct, a feeling—and is generally mysterious in its workings.

The Classical story accepts that no one ever fully understands anyone else; that there must be secrets, that there will be loneliness, that there must be compromise. It believes that we have to learn how to sustain good relationships, that love is not just a chance endowment of nature, that love is a skill, not a feeling.

We will know that we are finally ready for love when we have stopped telling ourselves the wrong stories and when some of the following requirements are in place:

1. When we have given up on perfection

It is crucial that we give up on the notion that life would be perfect with anyone; the best we can hope for is a "good enough" relationship. To force this truth into our brains, it is useful for a few relationships to fail before we commit for the long term. It is not that we're honing our vision of the ideal partner; rather, we're gaining first-hand experience of how even the most exciting and seemingly perfect people turn out to be frustrating and disappointing in some important ways.

2. When we despair of being understood

Initially, love involves a wonderful feeling that this other person understands us in ways no one else ever has—they are kind to, and welcoming of, lonely bits of the self. But this won't keep happening; large zones of our inner life will remain that even they won't be able to grasp. It's not their fault that they can't recognize or make sense of parts of who we are or certain of our needs. It is not that they are obtuse or not trying hard enough. No one can completely understand or be entirely sympathetic to another individual.

3. When we realize we are crazy

It is the opposite of what we expect. We are reasonable and pretty decent. The problem, we feel, lies with other people. Maturity means admitting that we are often idiotic: We have not resolved past hurts; we misconstrue others' motives; we are guided by impulse rather than insight; we are prey to anxiety. We are loveable idiots.

If we are not regularly and very deeply embarrassed about who we are, it can only be because we have a dangerous capacity for selective memory.

4. When we are happy to be taught and calm about teaching

The sign that we are capable of love is that we embrace the idea that, in crucial ways, our partner will be more insightful and sensible than we are. We admit that they have much to teach us and we are willing to accept the lessons with good grace. Around some important things they will be the teacher and we will be students. But the same must hold for us: we must be ready and willing to be a good teacher—patient, forgiving, and kind—to them. Good relationships are built around the idea that they are educational experiences for both of us.

5. When we realize we're not compatible

According to Romanticism, the person we should ideally be with is someone whose tastes and interests are very similar to our own. This seems to make perfect sense at first. But as time goes on, these overlaps of enthusiasm become less significant because the points on which we differ become more and more evident. What we should really be looking for is not someone whose interests coincide perfectly with our own (such a person does not exist), but one with whom we can handle disagreement and divergence in comparatively generous and astute ways. Prior compatibility isn't crucial, because it will be revealed as significantly incomplete. Rather, it is the capacity to work at becoming compatible that is the mark of the "right" partner.

The Romantic vision of love has been unfortunate: It sets up impossibly high hopes. Judged by that standard, any actual relationship will seem like a failure, thus promoting separation and breakups. We need to replace the Romantic vision with a more candid, realistic view of what "good enough" relationships are actually like, with all their normal stresses and sorrows. And we should provide ourselves with tools, in the form of ideas, stories, and jokes, that help us face the ordinary trials of shared life in a slightly more intelligent and less panicked way.

Picture credits

Cover	Douglas Adesko, represented by AMP Agency
p. 28	Rorschach test. Photo Researchers Inc. / Alamy Stock Photo
p. 29	Thematic Apperception Test by Henry A. Murray, Card 12F, Cambridge, Mass.: Harvard University Press, Copyright © 1943 by the President and Fellows of Harvard College, Copyright © renewed 1971 by Henry A. Murray
p. 93	Henri Matisse, *La Pompadour*, 1951 frontispiece of "Portraits par Henri Matisse" published by André Sauret, Editions du Livre, Monte Carlo, 1954. © Succession H. Matisse / DACS 2021. Photo: Archives Henri Matisse, all rights reserved

Also available from The School of Life:

The School of Life: Calm

The harmony and serenity we crave

A guide to developing the art of finding serenity by understanding the sources of our anxiety and frustrations.

Nowadays almost all of us wish we could be calmer; it is one of the distinctive longings of the modern age. Across history people have sought adventure and excitement, however a new priority for many of us is a desire to be more tranquil. This is a book designed to support us in our endeavors to remain calm against all the adversities life throws at us.

A calm state of mind is not a divine gift, we can alter our responses to everyday things and educate ourselves in the art of remaining calm, not through slow breathing or special teas, but through thinking.

This is a book that explores the causes of our greatest stresses and anxieties and gives us a succession of highly persuasive, beautiful, and sometimes dryly comic arguments with which to defend ourselves against panic and confusion.

ISBN: 978-1-915087-14-0
£9.99 | $14.99

THE SCHOOL OF LIFE

ON
BEING NICE

A guide to friendship and connection

The School of Life: On Being Nice

A guide to friendship and connection

A guide to rediscovering niceness as one of the highest of all human achievements.

Many books seek to make us richer or thinner. This book wants to help us to be nicer: less irritable, more patient, readier to listen, warmer, and less prickly. Niceness may not have the immediate allure of money or fame, but it is a hugely important quality nevertheless, and one that we neglect at our peril.

On Being Nice gently leads us around the key themes of the often-forgotten quality of being nice. It discusses how to be charitable, how to forgive, how to be natural, and how to reassure, as well as the importance of navigating interpersonal relationships with compassion and kindness. Ultimately, the book encourages us to understand that niceness is compatible with strength and is not an indicator of naivety.

ISBN: 978-1-915087-15-7
£9.99 | $14.99

THE SCHOOL OF LIFE

SMALL
PLEASURES

What makes life truly valuable

The School of Life: Small Pleasures

What makes life truly valuable

Explores and appreciates the small pleasures found in everyday life.

So often we exhaust ourselves and the planet in a search for very large pleasures, while all around us lies a wealth of small pleasures, which if only we paid more attention could bring us solace and joy at little cost and effort. But we need some encouragement to focus our gaze.

This is a book to guide us to the best of life's small pleasures: the distinctive delight of holding a child's hand, having a warm bath, the joy of the evening sky. It is an intriguing, evocative mix of small pleasures to heighten the senses and return us to the world with new-found excitement and enthusiasm.

Small pleasures turn out not to be small at all: they are points of access to the great themes of our lives. Every chapter puts one such moment of enjoyment under a magnifying glass to find out what's really going on in it and why it touches and moves us and makes us smile.

ISBN: 978-1-915087-16-4

£9.99 | $14.99

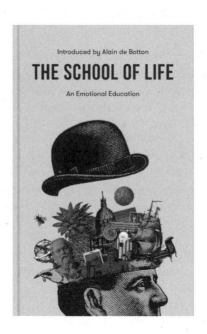

The School of Life: An Emotional Education

**How to live wisely and well in the twenty-first century—
an Introduction to the modern art of emotional intelligence.**

Emotional intelligence affects every aspect of the way we live, from romantic to professional relationships, from our inner resilience to our social success. It is arguably the single most important skill for surviving the twenty-first century. But what does it really mean?

One decade ago, Alain de Botton founded The School of Life, an institute dedicated to understanding and improving our emotional intelligence. Now he presents the gathered wisdom of those ten years in a wide-ranging and innovative compendium of emotional intelligence which forms an introduction to The School of Life. Using his trademark mixture of analysis and anecdote, philosophical insight, and practical wisdom, he considers how we interact with each other and with ourselves, and how we can do so better.

From the reigning master of popular philosophy, *The School of Life: An Emotional Education* is an essential look at the skill set that defines our modern lives.

ISBN: 978-1-912891-45-0
£10.99 | $14.99

Stay or Leave

How to remain in, or end, your relationship

A book to offer clarity and guidance when facing the difficult decision of whether your relationship has a future.

Whether we should stay in or leave a relationship is one of the most consequential and painful decisions we are ever likely to confront. What makes the issue so hard is that there are no fixed rules for judgment. How can we tell whether a relationship is "good enough" or plain wrong? How do we draw the line between justified longing and naivety? Does someone "better" actually exist?

All these questions typically haunt our minds as we weigh up whether to stay or go. *Stay or Leave* walks us gently through our options, opening our minds to perspectives we might not have considered. Using its lessons, we can understand ourselves deeply, consider our options, minimize our regrets, and find the way ahead.

ISBN: 978-1-912891-40-5

£15 | $19.99

THE SCHOOL OF LIFE

The Couple's
Workbook

Homework to help love last

The Couples Workbook
Homework to help love last

Therapeutic exercises to help couples nurture patience, forgiveness, and humor.

Love is a skill, not just an emotion—and in order for us to get good at it, we have to practice, as we would in any other area we want to shine in.

Here is a workbook containing the very best exercises that any couple can undertake to help their relationship function optimally—exercises to foster understanding, patience, forgiveness, humor, and resilience in the face of the many hurdles that invariably arise in a relationship.

The goal is always to unblock channels of feeling and improve communication. Not least, doing exercises together is—at points—simply a lot of fun. No one can be intuitively good at relationships. We all need to do some homework to become the best partners we can be.

ISBN: 978-1-912891-26-9

£18 | $24.99

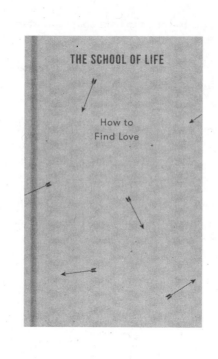

THE SCHOOL OF LIFE

How to
Find Love

How to Find Love

A guide to navigating the emotional minefield of love and relationships.

Choosing a partner is one of the most consequential and tricky decisions we will ever make. The cost of repeated failure is immense. And yet we are often so alone with the search. Partners used to be found for us by parents and society. Now we are expected to follow our feelings— and so locate people by ourselves, according to intuition. This should be an improvement, but our emotions often pull us towards hugely problematic characters and dynamics.

How to Find Love explains why we have the 'types' we do—and how our early experiences give us scripts of how and whom we can love. It sheds light on harmful repetitive patterns and the extent to which we are not always simply choosing people who can make us happy. In addition, we learn the most common techniques we use to sabotage our chances of fulfilment—and why, despite their costs to us, we unwittingly engage in them.

ISBN: 978-0-9955736-9-7
£10 | $14.99

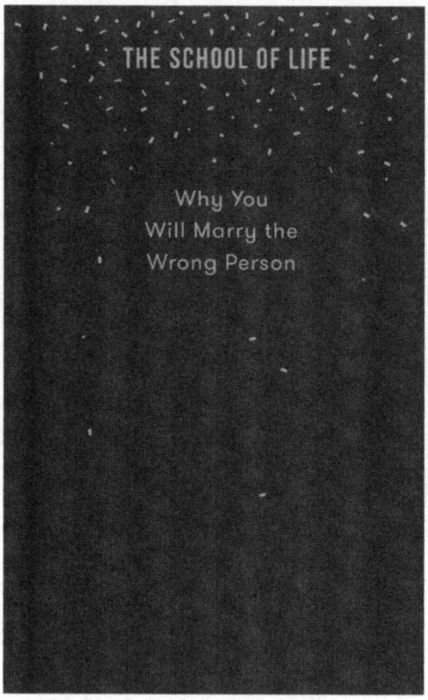
THE SCHOOL OF LIFE
Why You
Will Marry the
Wrong Person

Why You Will Marry the Wrong Person

A pessimist's guide to marriage, offering insight, practical advice, and consolation.

It's one of the things we are most afraid might happen to us. We go to great lengths to avoid it. And yet we do it all the same. We marry the wrong person.

Anyone we might marry could, of course, be a little bit wrong for us. We know that perfection is not on the cards. The fault isn't entirely our own. In the Classical age one might have considered criteria such as how much land a prospective marriage partner has. In the Romantic age, which still dominates our culture, we place great confidence in intuition—a sense that there is such a thing as "the one", that you understand one another perfectly and that you both never want to sleep with anyone else again.

The time has come to bury the Romantic intuition-based view of marriage and learn to practice and rehearse marriage as one would ice-skating or violin playing, activities no more deserving of systematic periods of instruction.

ISBN: 978-0-9955736-2-8

£10 | $14.99

The School of Life is a global organization helping people lead more fulfilled lives. It is a resource for helping us understand ourselves, for improving our relationships, our careers and our social lives—as well as for helping us find calm and get more out of our leisure hours. We do this through films, workshops, books, apps, gifts, and community. You can find us online, in stores, and in welcoming spaces around the globe. '